HANDBOOK
THE VOLUN

Second Edition

Sidney J. Rauch
Hofstra University

Joseph Sanacore
Hauppauge School District
Hauppauge, Long Island, New York

Editors

Published by the
INTERNATIONAL READING ASSOCIATION
Box 8139 Newark, Delaware 19714

INTERNATIONAL READING ASSOCIATION

Copyright 1985 by the
International Reading Association, Inc.

Library of Congress Cataloging in Publication Data
Main entry under title:
Handbook for the volunteer tutor, second edition.

   Includes bibliographies.
   1. Reading—Addresses, essays, lectures. 2. Tutors and
tutoring—Addresses, essays, lectures. 3. Volunteer
workers in education—Addresses, essays, lectures.
4. Word recognition—Addresses, essays, lectures.
5. Comprehension—Addresses, essays, lectures. I. Rauch,
Sidney J.   II. Sanacore, Joseph.
LB1050.H277   1984   371.3'94   84-15723
ISBN 0-87207-909-0

Third Printing, March 1987

CONTENTS

FOREWORD

Handbook for the Volunteer Tutor, second edition, replaces the first edition published by the International Reading Association in 1969. In the intervening fifteen years, many changes have taken place but a number of basic concepts and practices have stood the test of time. In this second edition, such a blending of the new and the tried provides an important source, not only for volunteer tutors but for tutors or trained educators in a variety of situations.

The first edition of *Handbook for the Volunteer Tutor* grew from the wisdom of Dorothy Kendall Bracken, president of the International Reading Association from 1965-1966. She appointed a volunteer tutor committee to 1) explore volunteer tutor programs; 2) investigate IRA's responsibility in this area; and 3) recommend ways of contributing if IRA recognized such a responsibility. H. Alan Robinson was appointed chairperson of the exploratory committee whose membership included Thomas Edwards, Jerry Parsley, Sidney Rauch, and Harry Singer. As a result of exploring programs and publications, the committee unanimously recommended that IRA publish a "booklet devoted to specific aids in reading for those people working in volunteer tutoring programs." The 1966-1967 Volunteer Tutor Committee, appointed by IRA President Mildred Dawson, and consisting of Sidney Rauch (chairperson), Doris Baxter, Thomas Edwards, Harry Singer, and Alfred Weinstein, played a major role in offering suggestions for the first edition. Sidney Rauch became the compiler and editor of the volume which featured chapters by Rauch, Thomas Edwards, Richard Carner, Samuel Shohen, Harry Singer, David Shepherd, Lenore Sandel, Lillie Pope, and Edward Summers.

This second edition of *Handbook for the Volunteer Tutor* is edited by Sidney J. Rauch and Joseph Sanacore, both of whom bring rich experiential backgrounds to the topic as editors, conceptualizers, and supervisors of practitioners. The array of talent reflected in the table of contents includes most of the original authors who were willing to give their time and effort in order to update the volume. They have provided the reader with numerous ideas and practical suggestions which can be put to use instantaneously.

The editors point out that the chapters were written for volunteer tutors who work with individuals in mind. Every attempt was made to keep the language simple and the suggestions specific. The editors have provided a glossary of terms. However, there are bound to be certain concepts that require further explanation. When possible, the volunteer tutor should seek the assistance of experienced teachers or reading specialists if further clarification is needed. Directors or coordinators of volunteer programs ought to take the time to introduce and explain the key features of the *Handbook* to the tutors.

Readers will agree that this book has continuity and unity of purpose, undoubtedly a result of careful editing and the quality of the authors' contributions. This second edition of the *Handbook for the Volunteer Tutor* makes worthwhile reading. More important, it serves as a valuable, functional tool of instruction for the volunteer tutor.

H. Alan Robinson
Hofstra University

AN OVERVIEW

This second edition of *Handbook for the Volunteer Tutor* provides suggestions for tutors who work with individuals. Most of the concepts, practices, and materials presented are directed to elementary and secondary school students who can benefit from extra help in reading.

Each chapter offers valuable information related to successful volunteer programs, but the reader of the *Handbook* is reminded that there is no best method. Although instructional approaches should represent sound research and practice, they also should reflect sensitivity to what works best for the student. The tutor must demonstrate intelligence, ingenuity, and warmth when attempting to reach individuals who are in need. Thus, the tutor increases the potential for helping each student attain success.

This monograph consists of nine chapters. While efforts have been made to achieve continuity and unity of purpose, the styles and ideas of individual authors have been maintained.

Chapter 1 provides a foundation for training volunteer tutors. Sidney Rauch discusses important qualities for successful reading programs and suggests topics to be considered for instructional sessions for tutors. He also stresses pertinent guiding principles that should be reflected in the training sessions.

Chapter 2 is updated by H. Alan Robinson, in memory of Thomas J. Edwards. This chapter has useful insights about establishing a positive tutor-student relationship. According to Edwards, students "need success, and they need someone who will provide and recognize success for them."

In Chapter 3, Richard L. Carner highlights the importance of evaluating students' reading difficulties. He describes aspects of group assessment, and he emphasizes factors involved in individual diagnosis.

Chapter 4 concerns basic teaching procedures to be applied during tutoring sessions. Samuel S. Shohen discusses functional reading skills, lesson plans, activities, and other important areas that can improve reading instruction.

The focus of Chapter 5 is word recognition. Harry Singer stresses aspects of teaching decoding skills and types of word recognition techniques. The author also presents a variety of cautions in teaching word recognition.

In Chapter 6, David L. Shepherd describes eight comprehension skills, discusses prerequisites to effective comprehension, and provides suggestions for teaching comprehension. He also shows examples of paragraphs and questions that foster skill development.

Chapter 7 concerns prior knowledge, writing, and metacognition. Joseph Sanacore discusses these areas in the context of theory, research, and practice. He also presents guidelines for improving reading lessons.

Strategies for organizing the volunteer tutor program are highlighted in Chapter 8. Lenore Sandel gives structure to the program by providing applications, an assignment sheet, a lesson plan outline, and a contact sheet. In addition, she describes aspects of Literacy Volunteers of Long Island, Inc., and she gleans from research concerning volunteer tutor programs.

Chapter 9 focuses on resources for the volunteer tutor. Dolores Weissberg lists an extensive number of materials and provides a directory of publishers.

In addition, the editors acknowledge the support of the following individuals who contributed their experience and insight to the first edition of the *Handbook*: Doris Baxter, Dorothy Bracken, Mildred Dawson, Rita Gold, Julia Higgs, Jerry Parsley, H. Alan Robinson, and Alfred Weinstein.

The editors and chapter authors of the second edition of *Handbook for the Volunteer Tutor* believe the ideas presented will help tutors work more effectively with individuals who need extra help in reading. The actual tutor-student instructional setting, however, is the real test. Tutors must be flexible in trying various techniques and materials for reaching individual students.

SJR
JS

A Glossary of Terms

The following definitions may be of value to the volunteer tutor. These definitions are adapted from Theodore L. Harris and Richard E. Hodges (Coeditors), *A Dictionary of Reading and Related Terms,* Newark, Delaware: International Reading Association, 1981.

Bibliotherapy: The use of selected reading materials that help the reader develop self-awareness and solve personal problems.

Bilingual: Ability to speak or understand, with some proficiency, another language in addition to a native language.

Decode: Identify words in a written message.

Developmental Reading: Reading instruction, except remedial, for students at all levels.

Diagnosis: The act, or result, of identifying reading difficulties; in education, diagnosis usually includes the planning of instruction based on the assessment of the learning difficulties and a consideration of their causes.

Dialect: A regionally spoken variety of a given language reflecting a different pronunciation, grammar, and vocabulary; dialect does not indicate a separate language, since there is mutual understandability.

Enrichment: Provision of additional educational experiences that supplement regular classroom activities; activities for the gifted and the disadvantaged; supplementary reading in the classroom.

Gifted: Having special skills or talents; having superior intellectual potential.

Phonics: An approach to the teaching of reading and spelling that emphasizes symbol-sound relationships.

Reading Comprehension: The process of understanding what is read; a presumed hierarchy of reading comprehension processes suggesting a literal level, an interpretive level, a critical or evaluative level, and a creative level.

Remedial Reading: Specialized reading instruction suited to the needs of students who do not perform satisfactorily with regular reading instruction; remedial reading is usually highly individualized and is often conducted in a special class or clinic by a person trained in specialized methods in reading; students reading below their expectancy are frequently eligible for remedial reading instruction.

Study Skills: A general term for strategies and methods that help individuals listen or read for specific purposes with the intent to remember. Study skills include locating, selecting, organizing, and retaining information; following directions; and reading flexibly.

Teaching Aide: A person who helps a teacher in instructional and clerical tasks; teaching paraprofessional.

Tutor: A person who instructs on an individual basis.

Word Recognition: The process of determining the pronunciation and some degree of meaning of words in printed or written form.

Chapter 1

WHAT THE VOLUNTEER TUTOR SHOULD KNOW ABOUT READING INSTRUCTION

Sidney J. Rauch
Hofstra University

Rationale

Volunteer tutors, with rare exceptions, are not classroom teachers, reading teachers, or learning specialists. Tutors may possess such essential characteristics as motivation, enthusiasm, and common sense, but they are not trained teachers. In many instances, tutors will be working with children, adolescents, or adults who require the services of a skilled reading specialist, but such personnel are not available. Can one afford to do nothing or just wait and hope for the specialist to appear on the scene? The answer is an obvious "No." There are thousands of persons who need immediate assistance, and volunteer tutors are the only ones who can offer the necessary reading aid. We must attempt to make the most of these dedicated individuals who have offered their services. But we must supply them with the necessary background information and effective teaching techniques. It is the purpose of this handbook to help develop *trained* volunteer tutors.

The Training Program

The average volunteer tutor possesses qualities that are basic to the success of any reading program: 1) a desire to help, 2) enthusiasm for the program, 3) a liking for people, 4) time to devote to the program, and 5) a willingness to learn. While these qualities do not guarantee the success of any program, no program can be successful without these qualities as a foundation.

Harris and Sipay (1) have pointed out

The most important single characteristic of a good remedial teacher is a real liking for children. The liking must be genuine; children quickly detect the difference between a warm, friendly person and one who puts on a show of friendliness without really feeling that way. Appearance, dress, age, speech, theoretical knowledge, experience—all these are less important than a genuine fondness for children as they are, complete with their faults and annoying habits.

This most important single characteristic—a real liking for children—applies to both the adolescent and the adult. In many instances, the understanding and sensitivity of the tutor to the problems of the adolescent or adult far outweigh that tutor's lack of knowledge about specific reading techniques. Many experts, in evaluating new reading techniques, have wondered whether the improvement has been due to the new techniques or method or to the amount of individual attention and interest given by the teacher to the child or adult.

But "love is not enough." Volunteer tutors must have some understanding and training in basic instructional techniques. They must also realize that there are serious limitations to what they can and cannot do. Thus, it is recommended that each volunteer tutor have at least 15 hours of instruction (preferably in five to eight sessions) under the supervision of knowledgeable personnel. One realizes that this recommendation is not always possible to fulfill, but it is made with the hope that certain standards will be met. Where possible, the training sessions should consider the following topics:

1. Basic Principles of Reading Instruction
   A. The nature of the reading process
   B. Why pupils succeed or fail in reading
   C. Expectations and limitations of the volunteer tutor
2. Simple Diagnostic Techniques (See Chapter 3)
   A. Use of basic word lists
   B. Informal reading inventories
   C. Phonic inventories
3. The Fundamentals of Reading
   A. Word recognition techniques
   B. Basic comprehension skills
4. The Study Skills (with application to specific, immediate problems)
   A. Basic reference skills
   B. Consumer skills

C. Forms and applications in everyday life
5. Personal or Recreational Reading
   A. Recognition and understanding of reading interests
   B. Sources of "high-interest, low-vocabulary" books (see Chapter 9)
   C. Library resources
6. Case Studies
   A. Descriptions of persons who seek help
   B. Representative cases to show what can be done
   C. Analysis of successful aspects of instruction
7. Representative Lessons (see chapters 4, 5, 6)
   A. For word recognition activities
   B. For comprehension skills
   C. For study skills
   D. For motivating the reluctant reader
8. Methods and Materials
   A. Language experience approaches
   B. Directed reading activities
   C. Programed materials
   D. Use of audiovisual devices
   E. Teacher-made materials
   F. Word games

Guiding Principles

The following guiding principles of reading instruction should be kept in mind as the preceding topics are covered in training sessions.
1. Learning to read is a complex process, and no one has been able to describe the best method for teaching children or adults to read. Too many different factors are involved—intellectual, emotional, social, and physical—for any one method or procedure to fit all individuals. Therefore, tutors must be flexible in their approach, and the procedures must take into account the needs and interests of the students.
2. Reading is more than the ability to pronounce words correctly. Gray (2) and other reading experts have emphasized that there are four main components in the reading process: word perception, which includes pronunciation and meaning; comprehension of the ideas represented by the words; reaction to and evaluation of these ideas; and assimilation or integration of the ideas with previous knowledge or experience.

3. The more experiences an individual brings to the printed page, the better the chances for reading improvement. We now know that experience or prior knowledge determines to a large extent the amount of meaning a reader can obtain from the printed text (3, 4). The tutor must attempt to identify and relate the student's prior knowledge to the reading task at hand. The language experience approach (described in Chapter 4) will frequently prove helpful when the average textbook or workbook fails to motivate the student.

4. Successful instruction is based on careful diagnosis of the individual's academic and emotional needs. While the volunteer tutor is limited in this area, diagnosis of word recognition techniques and comprehension skills should be emphasized. Selected word lists and graded paragraphs (for testing comprehension skills) can be used by the volunteer tutor.

5. Marion Monroe, one of the pioneers in reading instruction, referred to the 3Rs of remedial reading—namely, *relationship, release* and *reeducation*. One must remember that "average" remedial readers are frustrated individuals. In all probability, they have been frustrated for years in attempts to improve their reading. Students need to feel that this is a new chance or fresh start and that no one is being prejudged. So the first important step is the *relationship* of mutual respect between tutor and student. *Release* means that the student is relaxed and secure enough to devote the necessary mental, emotional, and physical energies to the task at hand, i.e., learning to read. *Reeducation* stands for the teaching process which can be successful only if the previous 2Rs have been established.

6. There is need for a fresh and different approach to reading instruction. The usual reading texts and phonics workbooks frequently represent symbols of failure to students. Students probably have had some remedial instruction (without success) and need a new approach and different materials. One of the most frustrating things that can happen to a tutor is to have a student remark, "I've had that before." or "That's boring."

7. Begin teaching at the student's instructional level or below. This principle involves an understanding of the concepts of *instructional level, frustration level, independent level*, and *hearing capacity level* (see Chapter 3). Thus, one session should be devoted to the theory and use of the informal reading inventory. For purposes of assisting

the volunteer tutor in the use of informal reading inventories, the following references should be considered:

Harris and Sipay, *How to Increase Reading Ability* (7th ed.), Chapter 8; Silvaroli, *Classroom Reading Inventory* (4th ed.); Aulls, *Developing Readers in Today's Elementary Schools*, Chapter 14; and Burns and Roe, *Informal Reading Assessment*.

8. Assignments should be brief, concrete, and well-motivated. Opportunities for success, particularly during the first two or three sessions, should be available and evident to students. Students must see evidence of progress or the program will have dropouts.

9. Tutors' attitudes must be encouraging and cheerful. Their enthusiasm can be contagious, and students will respond positively if the general instructional atmosphere is an optimistic one.

10. Remedial instruction in the volunteer program has many of the aspects of a good counseling situation. Otto, McMenemy, and Smith (5) present a very helpful summary of the basic techniques of counseling that can be adapted by volunteer tutors. This listing is reprinted with permission of the authors and publisher:

1. Drop the authoritative teacher role. Be an interested human being.
2. Communicate by transmitting attitudes and feelings. Do this by being real; it is more effective than simply to use words.
3. Arrange the physical setting so as to be close to the pupil. Do not sit behind the desk, but rather share the desk by having the pupil sit at the side. This is a technique that good remedial teachers have long applied.
4. Talk only about one third of the time when the pupil discusses his problems. This gives him the opportunity to do most of the talking and shows that you are interested.
5. Ask questions that cannot be answered with yes or no. Instead of saying, "Do you like to read?" say, "What do you dislike about reading?"
6. Ask questions using the declarative tone of voice. Otherwise you may sound like an interrogator.
7. Do not interrupt the pupil when he is talking. This communicates that what he has to say is important. However, if he digresses from the subject, focus him back on the subject by saying, "How does this apply to the subject we started talking about?" or "What does this mean to you?"
8. Give the pupil silence in which to think. Realize that there will be periods of silence during which the pupil is thinking. This takes practice, for in normal conversation silence produces a feeling of awkwardness.
9. Move the focus from intellectual thought to emotional feelings when feelings are being discussed. Ask such questions as, "What does this mean to you?" and "How did you feel about that?" (See the following three techniques.)

10. Observe and interpret nonverbal clues. Notice when the pupil moves his body or cries or drums his fingers. It is important to understand the relationship between his nonverbal clues and the subject being discussed.
11. Be alert to notice a change in the rate of speech, a change in the volume of speech, or a change in the pitch or tone of the voice. Such changes may indicate that there are emotional feelings connected with the subject being discussed and that the subject needs further exploration.
12. Point out what is currently happening. Say, "I notice your eyes are moist. What kinds of feelings do you have?"
13. Use brief remarks. Do not confuse the pupil with long, complicated questions or comments.
14. Pause before talking. The pupil may wish to make additional remarks; a pause of a few seconds enables him to continue.
15. Don't give lectures on ways to behave. Ask the pupil to suggest alternatives and let him make the decision. Help him to examine the consequences of his alternatives. Information, possibilities, and alternatives may be presented, but only for his consideration. There is a big difference between telling a person what to do and suggesting alternatives.
16. Avoid talking about yourself and your experiences. Do not use "I" and avoid personal anecdotes. Focus on the pupil and *his* problems.
17. Clarify and interpret what the pupil is saying. Use such remarks as, "It seems to me that your mother wants you to go to college." At other times, make a summarizing remark. But make these brief interpretations *after* the pupil has presented his ideas.
18. Do not be alarmed at remarks made by the pupil. Instead focus on the reason behind what was said or done.
19. Do not reassure the pupil that things will be all right. This will be recognized as superficial. Look for ways to demonstrate change and progress.
20. Do not make false promises. Instead communicate a feeling for the pupil and a desire to see and understand his problem; but do not appear to be overly concerned or to assume his problem.
21. Do not make moralistic judgments. Instead focus on what is behind the pupil's behavior; ask yourself, "What is there about this person that causes him to behave in this manner?" As a remedial teacher, do not blame the student for his failures; try to understand why he has failed.
22. Avoid undue flattery and praise. Instead focus on why the student asks for an undue amount of praise. If a pupil constantly asks such questions as "Do you like this dress?" say, "Yes, but why do you ask?" or "Do *you* like it?"
23. Do not reject the pupil through your remarks or nonverbal clues, but instead attempt to accept him. Try not to show impatience; do not threaten or argue; guard against any act that might appear to belittle.
24. Refer "more serious" cases. A more explicit definition of "more serious" cases cannot be given here. The remedial teacher must sense his own limitations and seek additional help when he seriously questions his own competence.

Rauch

Summary

The purpose of this chapter is to stress the need and importance of *trained* volunteer tutors. While there are serious limitations to what a tutor realistically can do, particularly when working with severely disabled readers, we must try to give this person as much help as possible. So this chapter includes the rationale for the tutoring program, suggested topics for training sessions, guiding principles, recommended techniques of counseling, and reference texts for further study and advice. The chapter also acknowledges the dedication, zeal, and past accomplishments of volunteer tutors. If we are to assist the many thousands of children, adolescents, and adults who need reading help, we must encourage those tutors who volunteer their services and do our best to see that they are prepared for their jobs.

A Basic Reading List for the Volunteer Tutor

The basic criterion used in the preparation of this list was "Will this book provide immediate, practical help for the reader?" It is neither expected nor recommended that the volunteer tutor read every book on this list; that is not the purpose of this list. However, these books (with guidance from the reading professional) can be important sources of information for the problem or topic at hand. For example, volunteer tutors should be familiar with the tables of contents of these books. Thus, if they are interested in word recognition techniques, they can read more thoroughly those chapters which deal specifically with methodology and materials. If, on the other hand, tutors are looking for diagnostic procedures and tests, they will examine in a more diligent manner texts which cover that topic. In addition, this list can be helpful for those individuals or groups wishing to build professional libraries for their tutors.

VOLUNTEER TUTOR TEXTS

Koskinen, Patricia S., & Robert M. Wilson. *Developing a Successful Tutoring Program.* New York: Teachers College Press, 1982.

Koskinen, Patricia S., & Robert M. Wilson. *Tutoring: A Guide for Success.* New York: Teachers College Press, 1982.

Pope, Lillie. *Tutor: A Handbook for Tutorial Programs.* North Bergen, New Jersey: Book-Lab, 1976.

Sleisenger, Lenore, & Joyce Lancaster. *Guidebook for the Volunteer Reading Teacher.* Thorofare, New Jersey: C.B. Slack, 1979.

Smith, Carl B., & Leo C. Fay. *Getting People to Read: Volunteer Programs that Work.* New York: National Book Committee, 1973.

Tutors Resource Handbook: Assessment Items and Sample Lessons. Washington, D.C.: Office of Education, Right to Read Program, 1974.

READING TEXTS

Aulls, Mark W. *Developing Readers in Today's Elementary Schools.* Boston: Allyn and Bacon, 1982.

Burns, Paul C., & Betty D. Roe. *Teaching Reading in Today's Elementary Schools* (2nd ed.). Chicago: Rand McNally, 1982.

Durkin, Dolores. *Teaching Them to Read* (4th ed.). Boston: Allyn and Bacon, 1983.

Ekwall, Eldon E., & James L. Shanker. *Diagnosis and Remediation of the Disabled Reader* (2nd ed.). Boston: Allyn and Bacon, 1983.

Dallman, Martha, Roger L. Rouch, Lynette Y.C. Char, & John J. DeBoer. *The Teaching of Reading* (6th ed.). New York: Holt, Rinehart and Winston, 1982.

Harris, Albert J., & Edward R. Sipay. *How to Increase Reading Ability* (7th ed.). New York: Longman, 1980.

Heilman, Arthur W., Timothy R. Blair, & William H. Rupley. *Principles and Practices of Teaching Reading* (5th ed.). Columbus, Ohio: Charles E. Merrill, 1981.

Lapp, Diane, & James Flood. *Teaching Reading to Every Child* (2nd ed.). New York: Macmillan, 1983.

Otto, Wayne, Robert Rude, & Dixie Lee Spiegel. *How to Teach Reading.* Reading, Massachusetts: Addison-Wesley, 1979.

Ransom, Grayce A. *Preparing to Teach Reading.* Boston: Little, Brown, 1978.

Robinson, H. Alan. *Teaching Reading, Writing, and Study Strategies: The Content Areas* (3rd ed.). Boston: Allyn and Bacon, 1983.

Santeusanio, Richard P. *A Practical Approach to Content Area Reading.* Reading, Massachusetts: Addison-Wesley, 1983.

Shepherd, David L. *Comprehensive High School Reading Methods* (3rd ed.). Columbus, Ohio: Charles E. Merrill, 1982.

Spache, George D., & Evelyn B. Spache. *Reading in the Elementary School* (4th ed.). Boston: Allyn and Bacon, 1977.

Stoodt, Barbara D. *Reading Instruction.* Boston: Houghton Mifflin, 1981.

Wilson, Robert M. *Diagnostic and Remedial Reading for Classroom and Clinic* (4th ed.). Columbus, Ohio: Charles E. Merrill, 1981.

Zintz, Miles V. *The Reading Process: The Teacher and the Learner* (3rd ed.). Dubuque, Iowa: Wm. C. Brown Company, 1980.

ASSESSMENT TOOLS

Botel, Morton. *Botel Reading Inventory* (rev. ed.). Chicago: Follett, 1978.

Burns, Paul C., & Betty D. Roe. *Informal Reading Assessment.* Chicago: Rand McNally, 1980.

Dolch Basic Sight Vocabulary Cards. New Canaan, Connecticut: Garrard.

Ekwall, Eldon E. *Ekwall Reading Inventory.* Boston: Allyn and Bacon, 1979.

Jastek, J.F., & S.R. Jastek. *Wide Range Achievement Test* (rev. ed.). Wilmington, Delaware: Jastek Associates, 1978.

Johns, Jerry L. *Basic Reading Inventory.* Dubuque, Iowa: Kendall/Hunt, 1978.

Silvaroli, Nicholas J. *Classroom Reading Inventory* (4th ed.) Dubuque, Iowa: Wm. C. Brown Company, 1982.

Spache, George D. *Diagnostic Reading Scales* (3rd ed.). Monterey, California: California Test Bureau, McGraw-Hill, 1981.

References

1. Harris, Albert J., & Edward R. Sipay. *How to Increase Reading Ability* (7th ed.). New York: Longman, 1980, 342-343.
2. Gray, William S. *On Their Own in Reading* (rev. ed.). Chicago: Scott, Foresman, 1960, 10-12.
3. Sanacore, Joseph. "Evaluating the Teaching of Reading in the Content Areas." Paper presented at the International Reading Association annual convention, Anaheim, California, 1983.
4. Sanacore, Joseph. "Improving Reading through Prior Knowledge and Writing." *Journal of Reading,* 1983, *26,* 714-720.
5. Otto, Wayne, Richard A. McMenemy, & Richard J. Smith. *Corrective and Remedial Teaching* (2nd ed.). Boston: Houghton Mifflin, 1973.

Chapter 2
*THE TUTOR-STUDENT RELATIONSHIP**

Thomas J. Edwards

So you'd like to become a tutor, but you're not certain exactly what is involved. You've had no teaching experience, and you're not sure what to expect if you do eventually find yourself in a tutoring situation. Precisely, what should a tutor do?

Or perhaps you are already a tutor feeling your way, and you don't know if what you are doing is likely to be helpful to your student. You have willing "subjects," but you don't want to let the students down. Also, you want the students to succeed—whatever their goals.

Tutors on the verge of getting a student or tutors who are floundering need to consider and understand a number of things. True, there are many books on "remedial education" or "remedial reading" written by professional educators and psychologists, but these publications tend to be technical and are not really designed for people who haven't had special training and who, therefore, don't even know most of the jargon of these specialists.

The purpose here is to get the show on the road so that you and your students can begin to operate. You need to know the needs of your students and how to help them cope with their needs.

Students will need help in two areas of equal importance. One has to do with *feeling better about themselves* and thereby getting a new lease on life. Your students probably have experienced failures and probably are members of some minority group—an American black or an American with a Spanish speaking background or an American Indian or maybe a white from Appalachia or the deep South. Regardless, the students probably feel culturally different from the

---

*This chapter was reviewed and updated by H. Alan Robinson, in memory of Thomas J. Edwards.

mainstream of American life and somewhat out of things. They don't feel that they belong: their language (or dialect) is different and their experiences have been different. They are different, and these differences are mainly responsible for failure. You must know the student's background. And you must accept and respect the "cultural cocoon" in which the person has grown up, even though it may contrast sharply with your own. Students will not trust you in the beginning and, therefore, you must demonstrate that you are a "buddy," despite these cultural and linguistic differences.

If your students are "culturally different," you may be the first and only person from the mainstream who has ever helped or ever will help them gain entry into this mainstream of American life: the first and last chance.

While needing your emotional support, students also will need help in the second area—that of academic skills, the things that are taught in school. But these things, in turn, are based to a great degree on what students learn before coming to school and the supplementary support received at home.

Actually, there are two additional areas you should know about, although you can do very little (if anything) about them. These areas have to do with *native intelligence* and *constitutional* problems. As far as one can determine, intelligence has to do with the capacity with which a person is born that enables the person to learn, to reason, to solve problems, to be creative, and to do all the other things that an "intelligent" person is expected to do. There are many people, however, who are unable to do the things one expects intelligent people to do but who could if their environment had provided the groundwork and the stimulation needed for the development of intelligent behavior. So there are people who don't *seem* to be intelligent but who have latent intellectual capacity that has remained untapped. One of your major responsibilities, therefore, is to tap or unleash this intellectual capacity in order to help your student realize maximum academic achievement and productivity.

The primary point is that one doesn't really know enough to be able to differentiate between those individuals who are deficient in native ability and those who have grown up under the disadvantage of having been culturally different. Hence, we must respond to all students as if they are bright and will "come around" if we are clever enough to release them. They must have the benefit of the doubt.

There are also constitutional problems: children who are born bright or normal but who have some kind of special deficiency that seems to keep them from special kinds of learning. Learning to read is one of these. There may be very little you can do for these individuals. However, you must not assume that your students fall in this category and, therefore, throw up your hands before you have done everything within your means to help.

The essential point is that when working with a student one must assume that the person is equipped to learn but has failed because not enough attention has been paid to special learning needs that stem from inadequate or different kinds of experiences. It's not hereditary but environmental. And if one is creative and clever and compassionate enough, one will be able to reverse the effects of these negative environmental influences.

The Feelings of Students

How do these students feel about themselves? They probably feel they have no significant place in society. This opinion may have developed because they are members of a minority group or because their family has instilled this feeling in them or both. They also probably feel that they will never achieve very much because they have been convinced they can't, and also because they have not achieved much so far. If this be the case, they will not be motivated to achieve and will have given up by the time they come to you for tutoring. *They need success, and they need someone who will provide and recognize success for them.* A good tutor will recognize these manifestations of "failure expectancy" and handle them by providing encouragement, easy learning tasks, and success.

You may be from an ethnic group that is different from your students'. They may see you as a member of the very group that has rejected them throughout life. If this is the case, you must reassure and accept but not by stooping or condescending. Students will sense this approach and reject you for it. Rather, be as natural and as honest as possible. Recognize, too, that you may have hangups that may make it difficult for you to see your students as bright, normal, deserving human beings. Tutoring may be a learning situation for you and your students.

You must remember that in your "diagnostic getting acquainted" with your students (your constant diagnosis en route) you must be sensitive to the feelings the students bring to the situation. And you must accept and handle them. If you don't, none of the teaching techniques you attempt will amount to very much.

Students will come to you armed with many strengths but also with many fears and self-doubts. Recognize, encourage, and develop strengths, and help, gradually, to dispel self-doubts.

The students' feelings and self-concepts *must* be considered and dealt with if you ever expect to be a truly effective mentor who will help your students realize the self-fulfillment of which they are probably capable.

Why Haven't the Students Already Achieved?

As was mentioned previously, students are not likely to achieve if their self-concept says: "I can't make it. I'm too dumb. I ain't never achieved before an' there's no reason to think I can now. But, maybe if somebody helps me realize that I can. . . ." At this point the tutor enters the scene to try to change the self-concept.

It might be helpful to you to take a look at the background factors that are likely to keep a normally intelligent person from achieving.

Experience. Many youths from elementary school up to college who need to be tutored have had very limited or very specialized experiences. And these have not been the experiences that help one make it in school or on the job. An Appalachian boy who is an expert at trapping and skinning may never have seen a skyscraper or an elevated train or even an airport. Or a black girl from rural Mississippi or from a Harlem ghetto may similarly have had very limited experiences. As the sensitive tutor practices constant diagnosis en route, the tutor must be on the lookout for these gaps in experiences and provide for them through firsthand experiences or vicarious, secondhand experiences.

Mediation. Adult-directed assistance in children's attempts to learn, right from the earliest years, can be called "mediation." In the earliest days of the lives of many children this mediation is provided by parents or older siblings. They talk to the children, explain things, answer questions, pose questions to make them think, read to them, and expose them to ever-increasing amounts of language. This kind of mediation helps young learners make sense out of the raw data of their experiences. And in the process they learn to perceive and interpret with greater precision and develop the language tools to help them communicate about new experiences and new understandings or concepts. The question is whether your students have had enough of this mediation to stimulate thinking skills and language development.

When children enter school, the teacher begins to assume responsibility for continued and somewhat more formal and organized mediation in the expansion of thinking and language and in the acquisition of additional information or concepts. However, if your students grew up in an environment considerably different from the average and did not have the amount or kind of mediation necessary for school success, they probably encountered immediate and continued difficulty in school. And many teachers from middle-class backgrounds often are not sensitive to the learning problems caused by cultural difference. So the problem continued until now you have stepped into the role of mediator as the learner's tutor.

Repertoire of concepts. You are trying to explain something new to your students—a new concept. The students have trouble understanding it. Why? It is quite possible that they don't already have the prerequisite background of conceptual elements to help in understanding the new concept you are trying to teach. It is rather difficult to teach a somewhat complicated concept like "topography," for example, to a ghetto-dwelling boy who has never seen a mountain or a plateau or an ocean.

In the event that your students have such concept deficiency, it is necessary for the tutor to be constantly on guard to sense these missing concept pieces and fill in the gaps before attempting to teach something new. Again, it's a matter of continuous diagnosis during the tutoring situation and taking care of learning problems as they arise. The effective tutor-mediator practices this diagnosis en route and provides for all of the learning needs that are evidenced; then students begin to succeed.

Oral language facility. Language is the major medium through which learning takes place. Learners *listen* to language as new information or concepts are being taught. Learners *speak* in attempts to demonstrate learning or to raise questions for further clarification. Students spend much time *reading* to expand their repertoires of knowledge or concepts from information contained on the printed page. And students *write* for the purpose of indicating what has been learned or to communicate new ideas or feelings.

Facility in handling oral language—listening and speaking—is rather essential to success in written communication—reading and writing. In working with your students, you should be assessing oral language facility continuously. This assessment is based on a number of specific questions you should keep in mind. It might be helpful to list them:

Edwards

1. Do the students have the necessary *information* or *concepts* required for communicating in an oral language situation? It is difficult to communicate if you have nothing to communicate about.
2. Do the students have the *vocabulary* or *spoken labels* for the concepts that may already have been learned? They may either be lacking this vocabulary or may have learned different labels for a given set of concepts because they have grown up in a special language environment with its own dialect.
3. Have the students developed *auditory perception* that would permit the grasping and reproducing of the speech sounds of so-called standard American English? One *learns* to perceive the speech sounds to which one has become accustomed. When one encounters unfamiliar speech sounds, one tends to distort them in the perceptual process and change them somewhat so that they fit more comfortably into the more familiar speech-sound system. Hence, an individual from a Spanish speaking background may not be accustomed to perceiving or pronouncing the short *i* sound, as in "hit," because that sound is not within the Spanish speech-sound system. Consequently, the student *mis*perceives it and pronounces it "heet." This kind of a problem with auditory perception will not only result in distorted pronunciation but also may cause problems in sounding out new words in reading and in representing spoken sounds in spelling situations.
4. Do the students have reasonable mastery of *syntax* or the way one customarily puts words together in sentences? Again, because of the dialectical cocoon in which the individual may have grown up, the learner may have become accustomed to a different syntactical system from that of standard American English. This difference may reflect itself in spoken and written English.
5. How about students' *language usage*? This area deals with points of traditional English grammar. Although various dialects permit perfectly adequate communication within a given linguistic environment, marked deviation from grammatical standards may cause breakdown in the communicative process. Further, the user of nonstandard language may be ridiculed, stigmatized, ostracized, and penalized in academic situations as well as job arena.

A significant function of the tutor is to make constant assess-ments of students' oral language facilities. Attempts to help students become proficient in handling standard American English must be casual so the individuals do not become self-conscious or inhibited to the point that they simply refuse to communicate. A dialect is not bad, only different. Students should feel free to continue using their own dialects whenever it is appropriate but should know when it is not appropriate and should have alternative language options.

Reading and writing facility. Written language is the area in which there is likely to be the greatest amount of emphasis in most tutorial programs. This work is important but must be seen as only one aspect of a total cluster of needs that a given individual is likely to have. And the tutor must realize also that difficulties with reading and writing might stem from one or more of the problems mentioned previously in this chapter. Hence, it is imperative that the tutor see the interaction among a complex of needs and remain alerted simultaneously to as many as possible.

Regardless of age, students may manifest specific reading and writing difficulties characteristic of all age levels. The tutor must recognize the fact that reading and writing comprise a complex of interrelated abilities, and must be prepared to diagnose and remedy diversified difficulties as they arise in the tutoring situation.

Authors of other chapters in this book deal with specific techniques for handling reading problems. However, it might be helpful here to point out in a fairly orderly sequence the types of problems you are likely to encounter in working with your students. Again, this material might be presented most effectively in the form of questions you should ask yourself as you are tutoring.

1. What about student *attitude*? Are the students suffering from cumulative failures that have finally brought them into the tutorial situation? Are the students expecting more failure? Have they come to fear tasks that involve reading and writing? Do the students, therefore, need your constant support and encouragement as you teach specific skills? Are you providing learning tasks that will yield success?

2. What *background factors* are conspiring against success in reading and writing? These were mentioned previously and included the following: background of *experience*; repertoire of *concepts* that are derived from experience through *mediation; oral language facility* that would include vocabulary, auditory perception, syntax, and language usage.

3. Can the students *read* well? Reading itself is complex. Hence, one should ask a number of subquestions about student reading ability:
   a. Can students recognize whole words quickly, easily, and accurately as soon as they are encountered?
   b. When students come upon a word they do not recognize, do the students have the skills necessary to figure it out?

c. Can the students comprehend the meanings of sentences, paragraphs, or longer selections? More specifically, can they not only understand what the author states but also draw inferences, evaluate what the author has stated, and formulate their own conclusions?
4. What about your students' writing abilities? Writing is a complex act.
   a. Are the students able to organize ideas prior to the writing act?
   b. Are the students able to think through a first draft of writing and revise it with your help?
   c. Can the students edit a second or third draft so it is reasonably coherent and written with a minimal number of technical errors—spelling, punctuation, incomplete sentences?

Currently, there are numerous points of view concerning the most effective ways of teaching communication skills. In working with your students you may have to evaluate and select that method which seems to work best. You may even want to combine two or more methods. But the important thing to remember is that you will have to consider the variety of needs your students will have beyond reading and writing (the ones mentioned previously here) and provide for as many of them as possible.

Concluding Comments

If there is any single magic ingredient in the tutor-student relationship, it lies in the relationship itself. The cumulative failure the students will have experienced will be offset most effectively when self-confidence evolves from the awareness that, at last, someone cares how well they do and is available to provide specific help. Even if you make some mistakes in your diagnostic evaluations or in your attempts at remediation, the genuineness and the consistency of your concern will carry you over such humps. And it will be important to realize that your own native intelligence and creative attacks on the problems of your students will help you come up with certain innovative approaches that will be effective.

Tutorial programs are most important in salvaging much precious brain power and helping many thousands of young Americans realize self-fulfillment. So be proud of your volunteer efforts and more power to you.

Chapter 3

DIAGNOSIS OF READING DIFFICULTIES

Richard L. Carner
University of Miami

The original volume of *Handbook for the Volunteer Tutor* was published in 1969—the same year that a human being first landed on the moon. This event did indeed prove to be a "giant step" for humankind and demonstrated the human capacity to solve incredibly complex technical problems. Current available evidence, unfortunately, does not indicate that quantum leaps have been made in regard to significantly reducing the magnitude of reading problems over the intervening years.

In spite of the proliferation of teaching materials, systems, and computer technology, the need for remedial instruction in reading remains a high priority item for all age levels. The problems involved in creating a literate society are still with us, perhaps to an even greater degree than before. The relatively new dimension of "computer literacy" is having a revolutionary impact on us and has placed even further demands on the acquisition of reading skills. It is quite obvious that the computer will not obviate the necessity for learning how to read.

Some of the questions asked in the first edition of *Handbook for the Volunteer Tutor* are as pertinent today as they were then. The teacher is still faced with the problems of knowing the answers to: Where do I begin instruction? What are the major strengths and weaknesses of my students? What information do I need to have before I can begin instruction? Under what conditions should instruction take place?

While the questions persist, the answers may be almost as elusive as they have been in the past. Although we have not achieved the millenium, diagnostically speaking, we do have a variety of tools available to help us understand better the problems our students have.

However, one thing should be kept in mind by volunteer tutors. The testing they do should be both practical and appropriate. Such testing would *not* represent the kind of multidisciplinary, in-depth testing which is often possible within a clinical setting. The major purpose of testing done by tutors is to acquire specific information which will be of direct value in determining the strategies or materials to be used in the instructional program. Successful teaching often reflects the time and care taken by tutors in the initial evaluation and resulting planning.

Background Information

When tutors take on the task of working with high school dropouts or adults who have a history of failure in reading, it is important that as much pertinent information be accumulated as possible. Each reading problem represents a past that is unique. Therefore, it is important to gain some understanding about what experiences have led to success or failure. In every person and in every task there exists an expectancy for success or failure based on past experiences. Most high school dropouts or adults with serious reading problems do not enter into reading with enthusiasm because of previous failures. The teacher, consequently, must be aware of the negative feelings held toward reading. This atmosphere makes it doubly important to know the best place to start in terms of what is to be taught and what approach should be taken.

A careful investigation may yield much significant information concerning a student's development and patterns of achievement in school. Most frequently, school records are the primary source of information. Parents of recent school dropouts may also be of help in filling in informational gaps concerning the pupil. Basic areas of information may be summarized by a form such as the following:

Educational Background

Last grade completed _____ Number of schools attended _____
Grades repeated _____ Best subjects _____
Poorest subjects _____ Reading problem first noted _____
_____ What is current reading? _____
How much reading does subject do independently? _____
What was attendance record in school? _____

Previous Educational and Psychological Evaluations

Reading Test Results	*Gr. level*	*%ile*	*Date(s)*

Achievement Test Results	*Gr. level*	*%ile*	*Date(s)*

Intelligence Test Results	*Verbal IQ*	*Perf. IQ*	*Total IQ*

Previous Remedial Instruction

Agency _____ Duration _____
Type of Instruction _____
Results _____
_____

Current Reading Level

Informal Reading Inventory   Frustration level _____
                                    Instructional level _____
                                    Independent level _____

Standardized Tests (Name of Test)	*Gr. level*	*%ile*

Other Tests

Summary of Problems
_____
_____
_____

Program Recommendations
_____
_____
_____

Group Assessment

Although standardized reading tests can be administered individually, their major purpose has been to assess groups of students in order to determine reading levels. There are many reasons for their wide use and popularity. They are usually easy to administer; scoring may be accomplished by use of self-scoring answer sheets or machine; and they yield norms which are familiar and easy to interpret such as grade levels, percentiles, or standard scores. For a more detailed listing of such tests, the reader is referred to such sources as the fourth edition of *Diagnostic and Remedial Reading for Classroom and Clinic* by Robert Wilson (Charles E. Merrill) or to *Teacher's Directory of Reading Skill Aids and Materials* by Emerald Dechant (Parker Publishing Company).

The most commonly used standardized tests tend to emphasize two areas considered to be of importance when measuring or assessing reading levels: vocabulary (word meanings) and comprehension. A few tests attempt to provide some indication of the reading rate. Usually, this is accomplished by merely noting the number of words an individual reads in the first minute. However, this is usually done without any attempt to determine comprehension over this span of time. The value of acquiring information concerning rate without any accompanying assessment of comprehension appears to have limited value from a diagnostic point of view. Speed of reading should not be separated from the concept of *efficiency* in reading which is concerned with not only how many words are processed per unit of time but also how much is understood.

The usual means of testing is through the use of multiple choice questions—a situation which frequently invites guesswork and the possibility of results which, at times, can be highly misleading.

A case in point is a high school student who visited the University of Miami Reading Clinic for diagnosis. Because he was seventeen years old and a junior in high school, a well-known standardized test was used for the initial testing. The results showed that he was reading on the 9.7 grade level—considerably below his actual grade level. However, in the course of administering a word recognition test, it was discovered that he did not recognize all of the words at the *first reader* level. When asked how he was able to take the standardized test, he indicated that he had just filled in the spaces on the answer sheet. Subsequent diagnosis revealed an extremely severe reading problem. In terms of measuring his actual reading level, the standardized test had *over*estimated it by more than eight years.

"Inflation" is recognized as one of the problems teachers have when they use the results of standardized reading tests. There seems to be a rather broad concensus that such tests may, in reality, represent a student's frustration level in reading rather than an instructional level. In order to get more direct evidence of this testing phenomenon, I administered the vocabulary and comprehension sections of the reading portion of one of the most widely used achievement tests both as prescribed and as an informal reading inventory. At both the fourth and sixth grade levels, it was found that the standardized norms had yielded reading grade level estimates equivalent to the frustration level when the informal reading inventory criteria were used. The average inflation for the grade levels tested was for fourth and sixth grades.

Another disadvantage of many standardized reading tests is that they have a limited diagnostic value. Since the majority of such tests involve silent reading, the tutor does not know the exact nature of the errors being made. It is not unusual to find students who achieve a relatively high comprehension score in spite of the fact that they have serious word recognition problems. The reverse situation also holds true. The real problems in reading may be overlooked if the reading teacher is only interested in the scores rather than in what an item analysis of the test reveals. As previously mentioned, guessing is always a possibility where multiple choice questions are used and the relatively high scores of standardized tests should lead to a cautious interpretation of the results, particularly in establishing the basic instructional level of the individual.

Since it would do little good to use a college level reading test for adults who have a reading problem, the teacher should be careful to select a test at the appropriate level of difficulty. Quite reasonably, one would expect to find their reading abilities to be more in keeping with elementary grade pupils (first through sixth grades) rather than the average adult or college student.

The Adult Basic Learning Examination (ABLE), published by Harcourt Brace Jovanovich (1974), provides a promising approach in testing older individuals who have had limited schooling. These tests measure the areas of vocabulary, reading, spelling, arithmetic computation, and arithmetic problem solving. Level I is primarily intended for those whose ability would be from the first through the fourth grade levels, while Level II may be used for those who would place between the fifth and eighth grades. Because the content of these tests is more mature, they are much more suitable for school dropouts and adults than the usual primary or elementary level achievement tests.

Individual Diagnosis

A thorough diagnosis of reading difficulties usually requires more information than can be obtained from standardized tests. As indicated previously, standardized tests can yield unrealistically high scores which could lead to questionable teaching objectives. One answer for this problem is to use an individual test that is standardized and yet provides a more detailed examination into various aspects of the reading process. Several such tests have been published and have been widely used in schools as well as in reading clinics.

One of the most useful tests of this type is the Durrell Analysis of Reading Difficulty (Harcourt Brace Jovanovich) which measures oral and silent reading, word analysis skills, letter recognition, phonetics, listening comprehension, and spelling and writing difficulties. Graded passages allow an estimate to be made of oral and silent reading levels as well as performance in other aspects of reading. The examiner should be completely familiar with the administration of this test since it is necessary to make on-the-spot notations during the testing.

Other recently published tests are representative of the informal inventory category. While there are considerable differences in the levels they cover and in the quality of passages, questions, and criteria used for determining reading levels, they have some important things in common. Most informal inventories have the major objective of providing a more diagnostic, in-depth look at how the reader is functioning during the reading process. Therefore, most informal inventories are individually administered in order to yield the kind of information which would be of most value in planning reading instruction for each individual.

Informal inventories also tend to provide the tester an opportunity to see how the student responds to isolated words, what kinds of errors (or miscues) occur in oral reading, and how accurate silent reading is. As can be seen, the tester accumulates an *inventory* of the types of problems a student experiences through the use of words and passages which extend over several levels of difficulty. Generally, the results provide the teacher with an estimate of the student's independent, instructional, and frustration levels in reading. This information is potentially the best source for planning detailed immediate and long range instructional objectives for the student.

Some of the newer tests available as sources for diagnostic information and which employ the informal testing approach are:

Diagnostic Reading Inventory, Jacobs and Searfoss. Kendall/ Hunt, 1979.

Analytical Reading Inventory, Woods and Moe. Charles E. Merrill, 1981.

Basic Reading Inventory, Johns. Kendall/Hunt, 1978.

Content Inventories—English, Social Studies, Science, McWilliams and Rakes. Kendall/Hunt, 1979.

Bader Reading and Language Inventory, Bader. Macmillan, 1983.

It should be kept in mind that teacher-made informal reading inventories also have been used with some success for many years to help determine the *independent, instructional,* and *frustration* levels in reading as a means of making an accurate selection of reading materials for the instructional program. This is particularly important for individuals who have experienced considerable failure in reading in the past and are in need of feeling that they *can* be successful in learning to read. Although specific criteria may vary from test to test in regard to what scores constitute the different levels, it is quite commonly agreed that these levels may be defined as follows.

Independent level. This refers to that level of reading materials which can be handled by individuals on their own, without help from the tutor. It is necessary to know what this level is in order to provide books or articles for reading independently. It is apparent that the best of instruction will do little good if there is no positive reinforcement or practice in the skills that have been taught. Many persons with reading problems have avoided reading since so much of it proved to be frustrating or had become associated with failure in school. The right combination of interests and materials at the proper level of difficulty will often serve to make reading a more pleasurable task and, hence, motivate the individual to read more.

Instructional level. This is the level at which students may, under supervision, read to extend their skills in word analysis and/or comprehension. Successful instruction is more likely to take place if the reading materials are neither too easy nor too difficult for the reader. Again, knowledge of the instructional level will help eliminate the guess work in selecting appropriate materials for instruction.

Frustration level. This is the level which is too difficult for the student. It is obvious that the tutor must avoid the use of reading materials which are too complex and frustrating. A fundamental need for all individuals who have serious reading problems is to prove to themselves that they *can* succeed in reading. It is highly doubtful that feelings of success will result from reading materials at the "frustration" level.

One of the major reasons for establishing the independent, instructional, and frustration levels is to pave the way for intelligent planning. When properly administered, the Informal Word Recognition Inventory and the Informal Reading Inventory will help the teacher focus on the word analysis and comprehension skills that need immediate attention.

Informal Word Recognition Inventory

An important part of the total inventory is a simple test of sight words in isolation. This list may be a teacher-made one derived from books of a known reading level (such as basal readers) and should be representative of the vocabulary to be found in such books from the preprimer level through the sixth or seventh grade level. Usually, each reader lists all the new words introduced at that level in the back of the book or in the teacher's guidebook. A random sample for a list of twenty representative words may be created by simply dividing the number of words required for the list into the total number of words available at a particular level. Thus, if there were 300 words in all, every fifteenth word would be selected. In general, proper names would be omitted with the word either preceding or following the proper name selected instead.

Administering the IWRI

The first step in giving the word recognition test is to expose each word for approximately one-half second to determine if word recognition at a given level is automatic and accurate. Exposure may be accomplished by using an index card to expose and cover each word. If the word is known, the next word is exposed in the same manner until a wrong response is given or an unknown word is met. The word is then presented in an untimed way for analysis. The examiner should record all responses to the word for both the flash and untimed exposures.

There may be occasions when it is advisable to check on word meanings as well as pronunciations. This check will give the examiner some idea about the vocabulary level of the student being tested. Also, when the response is difficult to understand, the pupil should be asked to use the word in a sentence. The following suggested scoring system and word lists illustrate the kinds of errors which can be made and the method of recording and scoring such errors.

Notations for scoring

1. hesitation: h
2. incorrect response:—
3. correct response: ✓
4. correct word meaning: m+
5. incorrect word meaning: m-

6. correct sentence usage: s+
7. incorrect sentence usage: s-
8. unknown part: (p l)a n
9. known part: p l a n

Word List (2nd grade)	*Flash*	*Untimed*
1. stories	*store*	✓
2. fall	✓	
3. almost	*about*	✓
4. tail	✓	
5. fine	✓	
6. watched	*watch*	✓
7. steps	*h*	✓
8. sleds	✓	
9. king	✓	
10. circus	✓	
11. penny	✓	
12. nearer	✓	
13. lot	✓	
14. above	✓	
15. puppet	✓	
16. bought	*brought*	—
17. ten	✓	
18. couldn't	✓	
19. beauty	✓	
20. feather	✓	
Percent Correct	*75*	*95*

Word List (3rd grade)	Flash	Untimed
1. seat	✓	
2. among	*along*	✓
3. plans	✓	
4. popcorn	✓	
5. (certainly)	—	*curtain*
6. (fawn)	—	✓
7. float	—	*flat* —
8. heart	*h.*	
9. feeding	✓	
10. bean	✓	
11. sleigh	*sl-*	✓
12. worth	*world*	✓
13. untruth	—	—
14. earth	✓	
15. giraffe	✓	
16. huge	—	—
17. decorated	—	—
18. sank	✓	
19. stubborn	—	*st, st-*
20. thick	✓	
Percent Correct	*45*	*65*

When the examiner finds that the untimed percentage score is less than 90 percent, it is necessary to drop to the next lower level or until all the words are pronounced correctly. In extremely difficult cases it is possible that some words may be missed even at the lowest levels tested. It is generally unwise to proceed with any list of words if the individual is obviously making more errors than correct responses. A sound approach is to begin at a relatively easy level and progress through more difficult lists until a score of below 90 percent is reached. An experienced examiner can reduce the amount of time required for testing by estimating the level at which to start. Quite frequently, it is necessary to give only three or four different lists to establish the range of word recognition skills.

Informal Reading Inventory

Both oral and silent reading skills are determined by means of the Informal Reading Inventory. The inventory consists of short passages at various levels of difficulty which may be taken from books of known readability levels. The passages should be of sufficient length and content to obtain a good sample of word recognition and comprehension skills at each of the levels tested. The results of the Informal Word Recognition Inventory should indicate the level of passage which should be given first. Generally, this means the passage will be approximately at the level where the individual has scored at least 95 percent in the untimed word recognition test. The range of passages, particularly with older pupils, may extend over a number of grade levels until the examiner has found the independent, instructional, and frustration levels.

The test should contain two passages at each level—one for oral reading and one for silent. It is usually best to use a continuation of the oral reading passages for silent reading since it will represent a more uniform difficulty level.

Administering the IRI

As in all good testing procedures, examiners should make individuals feel at ease. The purpose of this testing may be explained as a means of helping them with reading problems, such as a physician would diagnose a problem before writing a prescription. Disapproval or negative reactions to the responses of students should be avoided since this attitude may result in a lower performance than students are capable of making.

Making notation of reading errors as indicated, examiners should administer the oral reading passages first. Readers must understand that they will be asked some questions following the oral reading. Although numerous strategies for scoring are possible, the following have been found to be used quite frequently.

1. Phrases or word-by-word reading: vertical lines
   The | little bird | flew | away | from | its nest.
2. Omitted words or parts of words: circle
   The little bird flew _away_ from it_s_ nest. *went* *little*
3. Substitutions: write above the word
4. Additions: write in sentence
   The little *black* bird flew away from its *little* nest.

Carner

5. Repetition: a wavy line indicates portion repeated ~~~~~
6. Pronounce word if hesitation is over five seconds and place the letter *P* above the word. (Unknown proper names should not be counted as errors.)
7. Punctuation: write *X* in appropriate place (usually the period).
8. Hesitations: (over two seconds but under five seconds) place letter *h* above the word.

Numbers 2, 3, 4, 6, and 7 count as errors in which the percentage of accuracy for oral reading may be computed by dividing the number of errors by the total number of words in the passage. In addition to the errors which are counted, observational notes should indicate other symptoms of reading problems such as tension, nervousness, and evidence of visual, hearing, or speech difficulties. The comprehension score is the percentage of correct responses to the questions. The examiner should also be aware of the types of questions which seem to cause the most trouble (details, inferences, main ideas). In creating questions for the passages selected, the examiner should include questions which will reflect comprehension of the material rather than overemphasize the factual. Questions which may be answered by *yes* or *no* must be avoided unless a follow-up question asking "Why?" or "How?" is used.

Some of the newer informal inventories contain passages which reflect an appropriately low level of reading difficulty while maintaining a content which is more suitable to older individuals. The Bader Reading and Language Inventory provides passages which attempt to give older students reading material which is more mature while, at the same time, providing word lists and passages that are at lower levels of difficulty. However, teachers can accumulate a file of passages which would be appropriate for testing older students or adults by making use of a readability formula. A number of relatively easy to apply formulas are available, such as those by Fry and Raygor which can be used to establish reading levels of passages. Since basal readers are already written at predetermined levels, they provide another source for teacher-made informal inventories.

One of the most commonly used strategies for diagnosing comprehension difficulties has been to provide questions which reflect the kind of reasoning or thinking processes required in order to correctly respond. Informal inventories, either published or teacher-made, frequently label each question according to its type. Typically, the authors of such tests use *D, F* (Detail or Fact), *MI* (Main Idea) *I, E*

(Inference or Experience), *CE* (Cause and Effect), *C* (Conclusions), and *V, T* (Vocabulary or Terminology). Other labels for types of questions which have been used less frequently are *CRT* (Critical), *INT* (Interpretation), *LIT* (Literal), and *REF* (Referent).

It is usually best to record answers to the questions. Whenever the student gives an ambiguous answer it is appropriate to query further but not to provide any cues which would aid in giving an answer. For example, it would be permissible to ask "Could you tell me more about that?" or "Can you explain that further?" Unfortunately, some of the published inventories are vague in regard to what is an acceptable answer. Such a direction to the examiner as "Accept any reasonable answer" immediately leads to the problem of what is "reasonable." While it is important to test comprehension by sampling a variety of skills, it is necessary to have firmly in mind what an acceptable answer is.

The following samples contrast two informal reading inventories written at the fourth grade level of difficulty. Ostensibly, the passages could be used for either oral or silent reading. Preferably, a teacher should sample both oral and silent reading to acquire needed information. If there is a serious limitation on the time available for individual testing, it would probably be more informative to administer the passages orally in order to assess any word perception problems. The first passage is a teacher-made informal reading inventory and is based on an older Scott, Foresman basal reader series, while the other two fourth grade level passages are taken from the Bader Reading and Language Inventory (Macmillan). The first of the Bader passages is intended for children, while the second is more appropriate for older students or adults with reading problems.

Teacher-Made Informal Reading Inventory
(Upper Fourth Grade Level)

THE SEVEN DANCING STARS

A long, long time ago, when the world was young, a tribe of Indians dwelt in the midst of a forest. One day all the wild creatures disappeared from the forest as if by magic. Not even the most skillful hunter could bring home meat for the cooking pots.

The tribe roamed far and wide, seeking new hunting grounds. But wherever they went, the animals vanished.

At last Chief Big Hawk called his tribe together. Briefly he related what the Great Spirit had made known to him.

"The Great Spirit will lead us toward the setting sun," Big Hawk said. "Far beyond towering cliffs is a lake, the home of many beavers.

There we shall find fish that leap into nets as eagerly as bees seek blossoms. Bear and deer grow fat in the forest. Our cooking pots will never be empty."

So once more the squaws gathered together their few belongings. At daybreak the tribe set out for the new hunting grounds.

Questions

Det. 1. What people lived in the midst of a forest, a long time ago? (Indians)

Det. 2. How do we know it was a long time ago? (the world was young)

I. 3. Why did the animals disappear so quickly? (could have been a fire, a drought, sickness; enemies may have killed them)

I. 4. What weapons were used for hunting? (bows and arrows, spears)

M.I. 5. Why did Chief Big Hawk want his people to leave this land? (so they could find fish and good hunting)

Det. 6. Who told Chief Big Hawk where to go to find good hunting and fishing? (the Great Spirit)

Det. 7. What did he mean when he said, "Our cooking pots will never be empty"? (that they would find plenty of food to fill them)

Det. 8. What time of day did they start their trip to the hunting ground? (at daybreak)

Percent Comprehension _____ Time _____

Bader Reading and Language Inventory
(Fourth Grade Level for Children)

CHECKER GAME FOR KIM

Kim has an arm that does not work well. Sometimes Kim gets angry with her left arm because it doesn't do what she wants it to and accidents happen. When this happens, Kim gets mad and she calls her arm useless. Kim knows that with lots of exercise her left arm will work better and she will be able to do more things. Kim tries to exercise her arm as much as she can. Exercise is very hard work, but Kim keeps trying.

One way that Kim likes to exercise her arm is to help her dad make things in the workshop. She has fun working with her dad. They have just finished making a special checkers game. The checkers go into the holes in the board. This will help Kim. The holes will keep the checkers from being knocked off the board by her arm. She enjoyed helping make the game because she loves to play checkers. Kim likes to work with her dad and it is good exercise for her arm. (173 words)

Please retell the story.

_____ Kim's arm doesn't work well

_____ she gets angry

_____ because it doesn't work the way
she wants

_____ Kim calls her arm useless

_____ exercise will make it better

_____ exercise is very hard, but she keeps
trying

_____ one way to exercise is help
her dad in shop

_____ she has fun working with her dad

_____ What was the matter with Kim? (she
was handicapped, had a bad arm)

_____ What could Kim do to help her arm?
(exercise)

_____ What was Kim's attitude about exercise? (she knew it was hard, but kept
trying)

_____ What will lots of exercise do for
Kim's arm? (make it better)

_____ What was one way she exercised?
(worked with her dad in the workshop)

_____ What did they just finish making?
(a special checkers game)

_____ How was the board made? (holes for
checkers)

_____ Why was the new board good for
Kim? (she couldn't knock the checkers off the board)

Interpretive question: Why do you think Kim got angry and called her arm
useless?

(Fourth Grade Level for Adults)

LAND OF MANY RICHES

In 1869 the American Secretary of State, William Seward, did
something that many people thought was foolish. He bought a huge
piece of land called Alaska. He bought Alaska for only two cents an acre
from a country called Russia. But many people thought the purchase
was a waste of money. To them Alaska was just a useless land of rocks,
snow and ice.

However, the following years have proved these people wrong.
Some of the riches found in Alaska have made the purchase worthwhile.
One of these riches is the trees in Alaska's huge forests. Much of the land
in Alaska is covered by forests. The trees are cut and sold to all parts of
the world.

The sea around Alaska is full of riches, too. Many fish, such as
codfish, herring, crabs and shrimp live there. They are caught and sold
to the rest of the United States and the world. Alaska has been worth
much more than it cost because many riches have been discovered there.

(169 words)

Unprompted Memories

Please retell the story.

_____ in 1869 Secretary of State Seward

_____ did something people thought was foolish

_____ bought the land called Alaska

_____ for two cents an acre from Russia

_____ people thought it a waste of money

_____ Alaska useless land of ice, snow, and rock

_____ time proved they were wrong

_____ riches proved worthwhile

Comprehension Questions

_____ Who purchased Alaska? (Secretary of State Seward)

_____ In what year was the purchase made? (1869)

_____ What did some people think of the purchase? (very foolish)

_____ How much did Alaska cost? (two cents an acre)

_____ From what country was Alaska purchased? (Russia)

_____ Why did people say Alaska was useless? (covered with snow, rocks, and ice)

_____ What do they do with the trees? (cut and sell all over U.S. and world)

_____ What riches are found in the sea? (fish)

_____ What do they do with the fish? (sell them all over the world)

_____ Why was Alaska worth more than paid for it? (all the riches there)

Interpretive question: Why is it important for a country to have different kinds of riches?

Criteria for determining levels. Although there are many different ways of determining what the scores mean on informal reading inventories, the two major factors in deriving the independent, instructional, and frustration levels are word recognition accuracy in isolation and context and comprehension. These scores are usually determined for each level on which the student was tested with the word lists and the oral and silent reading passages. One method I have found to be effective in the scoring of an informal inventory is to average the *untimed* word accuracy for isolated words and the word accuracy in oral reading. The comprehension score is the average of both the oral and silent reading passages. These scores are determined for each level tested. Figure 1 illustrates how these scores are combined for establishing the following reading levels:

Independent—upper third grade level

Instructional—fourth grade level

Frustration—fifth grade level

Listening comprehension. An indication of the individual's capacity may be gained through a listening comprehension test. This test may be given by simply reading a passage of a known difficulty level and asking the pupil to answer the comprehension questions. The difference between the instructional level in reading and the listening capacity of the individual will provide some clue concerning the extent of deficiency that exists. Of course, this result will *not* substitute for the results from an individual intelligence test as an estimate of potential.

Figure 1
Informal Reading and Word Analysis Inventory

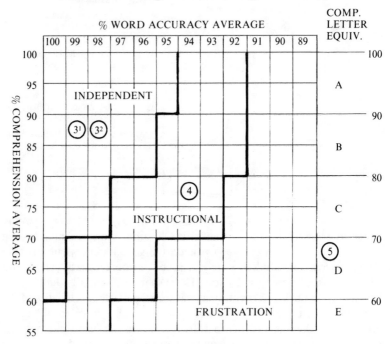

Carner

Level	PP	P	1	2^1	2^2	3^1	3^2	4	5	6
1	% Flash				100		100	95	85	60	
2	% Untimed							100	95	85	
3	% WAOR				100		98	96	93	89	
4	Average (2 & 3)				100		99	98	94	87	
5	Letter				A		B	B	C	D	
6	Oral-%				100		90	80	75	70	
7	Silent-%				90		85	90	75	60	
8	Average (6 & 7)				95		88	85	75	65	

Summary

Many tests are available to help the tutor determine the needs of pupils in relation to specific skills in reading, the level at which effective instruction can begin, and the extent of their reading deficiencies. Both standardized and informal testing procedures are desirable, but the strengths and weaknesses of each should be thoroughly understood. Supplementing the test results with anecdotal records or checklists will also help the tutor establish specific teaching objectives for each pupil. Testing should never become an end in itself but, rather, should serve as a means of creating an effective instructional program.

Chapter 4
BASIC TEACHING PROCEDURES

Samuel S. Shohen
New York State Education Department

This chapter discusses basic teaching procedures that can be used by the volunteer tutor. Since individualized instruction is strongly recommended for older teenagers and adults, suggestions are made for teaching sessions involving a tutor and only one pupil.

Developing Functional Reading Skills

Will your pupil become an excellent reader? The odds are against it. Generally, people with a long history of reading problems do not become good readers, even with intensive and extensive tutoring. Thus, your long range goal is to prepare your pupil for functional reading activities—the reading required to cope effectively with daily needs.

Functional reading activities can include:

- *Reading the newspaper.* Your pupils need to learn to read headlines, major news stories, want ads, general ads, and TV and radio listings.
- *Following directions.* Many daily situations arise where your pupil needs to read directions, e.g., to follow a recipe; to run appliances, tools, and machinery; to assemble furniture, toys, and other items bought unassembled; and to fill in various forms—job applications, driver's license and car owner-registration forms, and health and insurance forms.
- *Reading car manuals, road signs, and maps.* Perhaps your pupil wants to learn how to drive a car or possibly he/she already drives and even owns a car. Knowing how to read car

manuals, road signs, and maps is important to every driver.

- *Other everyday reading needs.* These can include the need to read personal and business letters; the telephone book; mail-order catalogs; the dictionary; receipts; monthly bank statements; and bus, train, and airplane schedules.
- *Reading career education materials.* Getting and maintaining a job is a top priority for many teenagers and young adults. The need to seek job information in articles, pamphlets, and books can provide strong motivation for improving one's reading ability.

Encourage your pupils to read beyond these functional activities to dip into popular magazine articles, novels, and the great literature of the past; but do not become discouraged if you fail to motivate further reading. Since your pupils never were readers, and probably never will become mature readers, be content if they learn to perform adequately in daily functional reading situations and thrilled if they begin to read more extensively.

Lesson Plans

Plan your lessons. If you are prepared with activities and materials for the instructional session, you increase the probability of having a productive lesson. At times, however, you might have to rearrange activities or capitalize on incidental learning situations that you had not anticipated.

Meet with your pupil as often as possible. Five days a week are ideal but often impossible to arrange. Two days a week are minimal; one day is better than none, but one session a week provides limited opportunity for reinforcing new learnings. Your chances for success increase with the number of times you work with your pupil each week.

Limit the lesson to 45 minutes or an hour. Much can be accomplished in this amount of time. Ideally, you want your pupil to want more and not become bored. Overworking even the most highly motivated person can be counterproductive, possibly leading to a breakdown in rapport and/or to unnecessary stress in the instructional setting. Remember, your pupil has failed to learn to read for many years. Obviously, you want *this* teaching-learning experience to be successful. Thus, the materials you select, the activities you create, and the length of a lesson are geared to maintaining a positive attitude and insuring success.

Activities

One activity or many can be included in an instructional session of an hour or less. The number of activities you provide depends on your pupil's attitude, attention span, and specific reading needs. No prescription can be written for you. Let your intuition be your guide as to how many activities there are and how long each one is. One specific recommendation can be made. *Stop an activity whenever your pupil becomes restless.*

You can find many good suggestions for activities in the teachers' guides and workbooks of elementary school basic readers. Although you might have to adapt some ideas for your older readers, you will find many activities you can use verbatim. Teachers' guides can also help you with the sequence of learning activities and methods of reinforcing new learning.

A typical lesson. A typical lesson can include a directed reading activitiy, an activity for developing a specific word recognition skill, and an activity for developing a specific comprehension skill.

Since methods and materials for teaching word recognition and comprehension are discussed in later chapters, only the directed reading activity (DRA) is presented here.

The DRA is the reading teacher's basic tool. By including one in each lesson, you help your pupil develop concepts and vocabulary, apply basic word recognition and comprehension skills, and gain practice in typical functional reading situations that will be encountered outside class.

A DRA is conducted whenever you want your pupils to read an article, story, chapter, or any other material at the *instructional level*. At this level, pupils need help in reading the material. If too much help is needed, the material is probably too difficult. Generally, readers are reading at their instructional levels when the following standards are met:

- Reads a selection orally and has trouble with only 1 or 2 words out of 20 running words.
- Reads a selection orally or silently and can answer 3 out of 4 questions asked.
- Reads orally in a conversational tone.
- Shows no tension in silent or oral reading.

Use the diagnostic procedures discussed in Chapter 3 to establish your pupil's instructional level. Then, provide materials at this level for directed reading activities. Published instructional reading materials usually indicate the reading level; however, if you use materials where the reading level is not indicated, judge the difficulty by the length of sentences and complexity of vocabulary. Generally, an easy selection contains short sentences and simple words; a hard selection contains long sentences and abstract words.

With the help you give, by the end of a DRA, your pupil should be able to recognize all words in the selection and understand the material completely.

Before undertaking a DRA, read the material yourself to identify the concepts and vocabulary that your pupil might not understand. Since printed words mean nothing until the reader brings meaning to them, your responsibility in a DRA is to help build your pupil's fund of prior knowledge that can be drawn on while reading. (See Chapter 7 for more discussion on prior knowledge.) In addition, by reading the material before presenting it, you can decide whether you want the reader to read the material completely or in parts, and you can develop questions to ask when guiding the reading experience.

There are 5 steps in a DRA:

1. Readiness
2. Guided *silent* reading
3. Discussion
4. Silent and/or oral rereading
5. Follow up

To conduct a DRA on an article, essay, story or chapter, follow these suggestions.

Step one. Develop readiness.

- Try to interest your pupil in the material by starting a discussion with a question that begins like, "Did you ever...?" "How do you feel about...?" "What would you do if...?" "What do you know about...?"

- Ask additional questions to discover what your pupil knows or does not know about the subject. These questions help you identify the gaps in your pupil's prior knowledge, and help you determine the information or experiences you need to supply to help the reader bring meaning to the printed page.

- Use a *brainstorming* technique during this question-asking segment to increase your pupil's attention and to provide additional contact with the printed word. As your pupil responds to your questions, record the answers in brief phrases or single words on a chalkboard or a large piece of paper. Accept all responses whether correct or not. Later in the DRA, your pupil can refer to this record to compare how well it matches the actual ideas in the selection.

- Introduce concepts and vocabulary needed to understand the selection. To clarify certain ideas, you might have to draw a diagram, show a picture, or use some other audiovisual aid. At times, it might be necessary to create an experience involving taste, smell, or touch.
- Write the "new" words on the chalkboard or the paper when you introduce them.

Step two. Guide the *silent* reading. The material should be read silently, *not orally,* which allows your pupil to read more rapidly in a manner characteristic of daily reading situations. While reading silently, your pupil also has an opportunity to use word attack skills without expressed effort.

- Ask a specific question (or questions) to establish a purpose for reading. Ideally, the best question encourages readers to think and to make their own predictions.

  "Who do you think...?"
  "Why do you think...?"
  "When do you think...?"
  "What do you think...?"
  "Where do you think...?"
  "How do you think...?"

  Then you can say, *Read to find out if you are right.*
- Have your pupils read silently to find the answer to your question or to confirm or reject their predictions. How far readers read depends on the purpose established and the nature of the material; readers might have to read one word, one sentence, one paragraph, one page, or the entire selection.
- If your pupils have difficulty with a word while reading, encourage them to use these strategies in the following order:
  1. Omit the word and reread the entire sentence.
  2. Use picture clues, if available.
  3. Sound out the word.
  4. Ask the tutor for help.

Essentially, you are encouraging your pupil to make a genuine effort to figure out the unknown word before asking for help.

Step three. Discuss pupils' answers.

- See if your pupils can supply the answers to your question or if they can respond to their predictions without your repeating the original purpose for reading; you are trying to train your pupils to remember the purpose for reading, which aids comprehension.

You might ask:
"What did you find out?"
"Were you right?"
"What do you think now?"
"Does what you read match what was listed on the chalkboard?"

- Ask additional questions, whenever appropriate, to stimulate thinking. These questions can involve facts, inferences, conclusions, and vocabulary meanings.

Step four. Provide for silent and/or oral rereading. Possible reasons for having your pupils reread are:

- To read a part to prove their answers to a question you asked.
- To read a part that verifies a prediction they made.
- To enjoy again the "funny" part or the "sad" part.
- To check on success in applying word analysis skills.

(If you divide the selection into parts, repeat steps two, three, and four until your pupils finish the material.)

Step five. Provide follow-up activities. The DRA is a valuable diagnostic tool. By observing your pupils' performances, you can identify their strengths and weaknesses and use these findings to develop follow-up activities to extend learnings or clear up difficulties. Activities can include additional reading materials, workbook exercises, teacher-prepared exercises, a drawing, or a quiz.

The steps in a DRA can be used to develop your pupils' functional reading skills. Readiness, guided silent reading, discussion, silent and/or oral rereading, and follow up are needed when you help them with newspaper articles, want ads, directories, and TV and radio listings.

Monitoring for Comprehension

The reading process is not complete until readers understand what the author has said. Your pupils should develop self-awareness and monitor their reading to determine whether they are comprehending. Monitoring can be accomplished by readers periodically asking themselves questions, such as:

"Do I understand this?"
"Does this make sense?"
"Does this sound right?"

If the answer is *no* to the self-checking question, the reader then has to ask, *What do I have to do to understand this?* Possible answers are:

Reread what I just finished.

Read ahead.

Look up this word in the dictionary.

Ask my tutor for help.

Although all mature readers might not monitor their reading in this fashion, learning how to monitor one's reading by self-checking can be an effective strategy for your pupil. An excellent way to teach your pupils how to do the self-checking is to model the desired behavior for them. For example, you can say:

This is what I would say to myself.

This is how I would think if I didn't understand this.

These are the steps I would go through in my thinking if I had to do this exercise.

Let me share with you the thinking I did when I read this.

Capitalize on opportunities to model the monitoring strategy and, whenever possible, encourage your pupils to describe to you, step-by-step, the thinking they do to ensure that comprehension is taking place. Ideally, you want your pupils to internalize the process and use it automatically while reading. (More on monitoring and metacognition can be found in Chapter 7.)

Review and Drill

Through diagnostic testing and observing your pupils' reading when working with them, you will become aware of weaknesses. Although you can give much immediate help during a DRA, it might be necessary to provide review and drill activities to reinforce certain basic words or skills. As suggested before, you can get many ideas for such activities from teacher guides and workbooks of elementary school basic readers. Use these ideas to create review and drill materials to meet your pupils' needs.

Psychologists report the greatest rate of forgetting takes place 24 hours after something new is learned. A person continues to forget after that time, but the rate is not so rapid. Therefore, it is important for you to provide review of a new learning in the next lesson. (If the next lesson is the next day, all the better.) If your pupils *understand* a new concept, new word, or new approach, do not assume it has been learned. Pupils need a review in the next lesson and probably a review periodically after that.

Do not overdo drill on lists of words. Review of new words is much more effective when the words are used in sentences. A good exercise might include a list of new words followed by a list of sentences with a blank space in each. Pupils have to read the sentences and write in the appropriate word. Such an activity provides meaningful contextual application instead of meaningless drill. (This exercise is illustrated later in the section, "Examples of an Experience Story.")

Review and drill activities will help your pupils refine their basic skills. Be careful, however, not to overdo this aspect of the program. It is possible for pupils to drill on main ideas, syllabication, and sequence of ideas but fail to apply these skills to their daily reading activities because there is an overemphasis on the isolated skill and little application of it to real reading situations.

Too much isolated drill and little integration and application to the total process can be illustrated by a basketball coach and his/her team. Suppose on Monday, the coach demonstrates how to dribble the ball; on Tuesday, how to pass the ball; on Wednesday, how to shoot the ball for the basket; and on Thursday, how to rebound if a shot is missed. Each day the team members learn their skills well, yet on Friday they play another team, only to lose badly. Although they can dribble, pass, shoot, and retrieve the ball, they still lose because the coach never gave them a chance to put these skills together in a practice game. The same thing can happen with your pupils if you overdo isolated drill. Get your pupils into the "game." Provide opportunities to apply all their skills to paragraphs, stories, chapters, articles, and books.

Language Experience Approach

You might have a problem finding appropriate reading materials for your pupils. Although many publishers have developed high level interest materials written simply, you may be unable to obtain them because of lack of time or money. (See Chapter 9 for lists of recommended materials.) Whether you have appropriate material or not, you can use a language experience approach to capitalize on your pupils' experiences and interests to develop their own reading materials. This approach has been used by teachers for years, and it can be very successful with older, disabled readers.

In a language experience approach, the pupils' own language is recorded by the tutor. Obviously, the pupils' words and sentence structure are familiar because they use them freely when speaking. This familiarity aids in reading the same words. Since your pupils' own spoken language is written down for them to read, no attempt is made to control the words or sentences. There are times, however, when you will need to suggest word or grammatical changes to help pupils express their ideas more clearly.

Frequently, you will find your pupils lack extensive word analysis skills to read certain published materials but they can read words that are self-dictated. Of course, rote memory is a fact in the language experience approach, but your pupils are almost guaranteed success, which is vital to building self-confidence. You can diminish the rote memory factor by using words from your pupils' experience stories in new stories and exercises that you prepare as follow-up activities.

Sources for Stories

Everyday activities offer a never-ending source of material for language experience stories. Encourage your pupils to tell you about happenings in their lives: a new job, last night's TV movie, a recent trip, repairing a carburetor, a problem with a friend, future plans.

Interests provide another source of material. Your pupils might be interested in a variety of subjects but cannot pursue them because of reading problems. Reference books, magazines (fashion, science, hobby, or sports), or anything written for the average adult reader present frustrating challenges. You can help by reading these materials to your pupils. Then have them dictate to you what they have learned while you write it down.

At times, you might lead your pupils into new sources of interest. You might find something in your own reading of newspapers, magazines, and books that you can share by reading the selection to them. This writer, for instance, has been very successful using *Life* magazine with adult pupils. (An example of an experience story developed from a *Life* article is described later.)

Steps in Developing an Experience Story

Using the pupils' own experiences and language, you can develop an experience story following these steps:
1. Discussion or research
2. Organization of ideas
3. Dictation
4. Rereading
5. Follow up

Step one: discussion or research. Establish and develop the topic for the story. If the topic is about an everyday experience,
- Encourage your pupils to tell you about it.
- Ask questions to draw out additional ideas or to help clarify thinking.

Shohen

If the topic has to be researched,

- Help your pupils find the source materials (encyclopedia, periodical, or book).
- *Read to them* the information needed, clarifying in your own words when necessary.
- Encourage pupils to tell you what they learn.
- Ask questions to draw out additional ideas or to help clarify thinking. (As your pupils become better readers, they will be able to do more of the research independently.)

If you want to lead your pupils into new interest areas,

- *Read to them* the material you have selected, clarifying in your own words when necessary.
- Encourage your pupils to tell you what they learn.
- Ask questions to draw out additional ideas to help clarify thinking.

Step two: organization of ideas. In this step you help your pupils select and organize the ideas they will use in the story.

- Ask questions, such as: "What ideas do you want to include?" "What group of ideas comes first, second, third, etc.?" "Do you need an introduction or conclusion?" "What is a good title for this story?"
- List or outline areas the pupils select:

    Carburetor
    Parts
    How parts work
    How to fix

    My Vacation
    Where I went
    Who went with me
    What we did

In a research project, you might ask pupils to tell you all they have learned in a free-flow-of-ideas (brainstorming) manner. Jot down the ideas without regard to sequence or relationship. Then you and your pupils can go through the listing to put together ideas that go together and to organize a proper sequence.

Step three: dictation. Have your pupils dictate their stories to you, sentence by sentence.

- Use the notes or outline developed in Step 2 as a guide.
- Print or type the story as your pupils dictate, having them carefully watch what you are doing.
- Say each word as you write.

- Help with sentence structure or grammar when necessary.

Step four: rereading. After you have printed or typed the stories, have your pupils reread them silently to provide the first contact with the written representation of their own ideas.

- Try to establish a meaningful purpose for rereading; direct your pupils with statements, such as: Reread the story to see if all your ideas are included. Reread the story to see if any corrections are necessary.
- Encourage pupils to ask for help if they have trouble with any word.

After the first silent reading, have the story reread orally, giving a second contact with the pupils' own words. Simply say: "Read the story to me. Let's hear how it sounds." Or you might have certain sentences or paragraphs reread for some specific purpose. For example, you might say: "I don't believe we've included all the carburetor parts. Read that section to me, and we'll see."

Whenever your pupils have trouble with a word during oral rereading, supply the word immediately rather than allowing them to stop to figure it out. Oral rereading should be in a smooth conversational tone. Remind your pupils that they should have asked for help with the word during silent reading. (The main purpose of silent reading before oral reading is to allow pupils to apply word recognition and comprehension skills at their own rate before being placed in an audience-type situation created by oral rereading.)

Additional silent or oral rereading opportunities can be developed in follow-up activities.

Step five: follow up. An infinite number of additional activities can be created from the original experience story:

- a story written by you using the same words from a pupil's story but in a different context,
- a word recognition exercise,
- a comprehension exercise, or
- a quiz.

Follow-up activities can reinforce your pupils' sight vocabulary and refine word analysis and comprehension skills. As indicated before, you can get many good ideas for exercises from teacher guides and workbooks of elementary school readers. Simply use the same ideas, but substitute the words from your pupils' stories.

After your pupils complete a follow-up exercise, have the responses read to you. This activity provides another contact with the words, as well as a check of the answers.

Example of an Experience Story

This writer once worked with nineteen year old Jack who had dropped out of school in the ninth grade. During the day, Jack worked as a helper on a county trash truck, but he was interested in going back to high school at night to get a better job to support his wife and six month old child.

Since Jack was reading at a third reader level, a language experience approach was used with him exclusively, including activities designed to help him fill in applications, read want ads, and use TV listings. He developed many stories based on his everyday experiences, and this writer created many follow-up stories and exercises from this material.

Jack subscribed to *Life* magazine, but he did not read it; he only looked at the pictures. One day he brought a copy to class to show the writer some interesting pictures in an article about the cheetah. Capitalizing upon this interest, the writer read Jack the article and following the steps outlined in the last section, the writer helped Jack create this story:

THE CHEETAH

The cheetah lives in central and southern Africa, just like lions. A cheetah cub lives with its mother until it is two years old. It grows into a very graceful animal with a small head for its seven foot body that weighs approximately one hundred pounds. Its voice sounds like a bird, and it can run over sixty miles an hour, making it the fastest animal in the world. Even though it can run fast, it can go only a short distance before it gets tired.

When a cheetah hunts it has to watch out for the bigger animals because they might take away its food. It hunts more by sight than by scent. After it gets its food and eats, it goes to a nearby stream and drinks. The dinner might last several days.

These follow-up exercises were developed from the story.

(A comprehension check, including repetition of important sight words.)

Directions: Read each sentence. Underline *Yes* or *No*.

1. The cheetah weighs seven hundred pounds.
   Yes   No
2. A cheetah cub lives with its mother until it is two years old.
   Yes   No
3. The cheetah runs over one hundred miles an hour.
   Yes   No
4. The cheetah gets tired fast when it runs.
   Yes   No
5. Cheetahs live in central and southern America.
   Yes   No

6. The cheetah's voice sounds like a dog's voice.
   Yes   No
7. The cheetah gets his food by smelling.
   Yes   No
8. Many animals are faster than the cheetah.
   Yes   No
9. Bigger animals might take away the cheetah's food.
   Yes   No
10. The cheetah's dinner might last several days.
    Yes   No

(A word recognition exercise emphasizing repetition of words and use of context clues.)

Directions: Put the right word in each sentence.

| head | cub | sight |
| scent | drinks | lives |

1. A baby cheetah is called a _____ .
2. Your _____ comes from your eyes.
3. Your _____ comes from your nose.
4. The cheetah's _____ is small for its body.
5. The lion _____ in the same place as cheetahs.
6. A cheetah goes to a stream and _____ after it eats.

Conclusion

The basic teaching procedures discussed in this chapter are by no means inclusive of all possibilities. You will get many more ideas in later chapters. Remember, you are trying to help your pupils succeed in functional daily reading activities. If you go beyond this goal and help them become real readers, all the better. But do not be too disappointed if you fail to achieve this secondary goal.

Be patient, your job is challenging and can be trying. You can be successful. Any sign of progress, as little as it might be, will be your greatest reward.

Chapter 5
WORD RECOGNITION

Harry Singer
University of California at Riverside

Introduction

Reading development through the grades. Learning to read consists of mastering three interrelated components: word recognition; word meaning; and reasoning about the meaning of sentences, paragraphs, and longer passages. In the initial stage of teaching individuals to read, the strategy is to emphasize only one of these components, word recognition or decoding. This strategy is accomplished by using stories that contain familiar words and ideas and stories that are interesting to students.

In the initial stage of reading development, typical learners usually have good control over their language ability; at the first grade, they have an estimated vocabulary of 2,500 to 7,500 words, pronounce almost all sounds well, use all parts of speech, implicitly apply the grammatical rules of their language, have accumulated some knowledge about the world, and can utilize all reasoning processes within their levels of cognitive development. Learners are thus able to communicate effectively with peers and adults within the limits of their experiences and intellectual maturity. Therefore, reading instruction can be and is based on this foundation of language, knowledge, and mental abilities. If the students are bilingual, deviate markedly in their language, have mental deficiencies, or are handicapped in some way, then other strategies have to be employed which stress language development and further simplify the reading task. However, for the average individual, the initial strategy is to emphasize the decoding process or recognition of words in print. By using reading materials with familiar word meanings and ideas with the experiences of the learner, students have only the task of learning to recognize words in print, use punctuation marks for pauses that occur in speech, and supply other speech components of stress, pitch, and intonation.

Word recognition is a complex task. Learning to recognize words in print or mastering a symbol system is not a simple or easy task. It consists of three factors: 1) learning responses to printed stimuli; 2) using one's language, background knowledge, and reasoning abilities to anticipate or infer words from context; and 3) integrating these factors into a synchronous, fluent, and automatic process. Undoubtedly, teachers do not remember how they learned to read. If they had no difficulties in learning to read, they might not be able to appreciate the complexities involved in learning a symbol system. To give the teacher some understanding of the complexities, the following sentence is written in a novel system that is probably no more difficult than the alphabet system:

$$(\text{٦٦F}, (\text{٦٦F}! \quad \text{Ⅱ LL}$$
$$\perp \sqcap \text{L} \quad \nabla \text{٦II}.$$

The above sentence, printed in the alphabet system is: *Look, Look! See the dog.* The key for this novel symbol system is printed below.

A △	H ⊓	O ٦	V ⊤⊤
B ☐	I ≡	P ⊏	W ⊔⊔
C Ⅰ	J ∓	Q ⊐	X ⊔
D ▽	K ⌈	R ▷	Y ⊢
E L	L ⊂	S ⊏⊏	Z ✝
F 7	M)	T ⊥	
G ‖	M F	U ⊥⊥	

Developmental changes in reading instruction. To teach individuals to recognize words in print and master the symbol system is a process that normally takes three to four years. Some students do so earlier and some later. But all students in the normal range of intelligence (IQ 70 and above) *can* learn to read, provided they want to learn and receive continuous and sequential instruction (*1*). As individuals learn to recognize words, their reading gradually shifts to more emphases on the other two components—word meaning and reasoning in reading or comprehending the printed material. Also, as individuals progress to increasingly more mature reading materials, they will encounter a corresponding increase in the difficulty levels of the vocabulary and ideas.

Individuals gradually reach a stage where they have mastered word recognition, usually about the fourth to sixth grade level. Any difficulties learners may have in reading at this time might be due to the vocabulary level or to ideas in the printed material that are too complex to grasp at their stages of mental development. For example, pupils might be able to recognize or sound out all the words in the following sentence, but not know what an essential word means and, consequently, not comprehend the sentence: After being in New York for a while, he began to understand the life led by troglodytes.

Learners could know all the words in the sentence, but still be perplexed by the meaning, as in the following famous sentence from Shakespeare's *Hamlet:* To be or not to be, that is the question. Consequently, reading instruction gradually shifts from learning how to read to developing the individual's vocabulary beyond the level of everyday use vocabulary, estimated at approximately 3,000 to 10,000 words, up to a reading vocabulary which at the college level is approximately 80,000 words. Also, the teacher of reading helps (along with teachers in the content areas) expand the individual's repertoire of concepts and ideas. Educators also guide students to infer or read between lines, to integrate background knowledge with text-based information, to read critically by drawing on knowledge and moral standards and criteria, to learn about style and literary devices, and to understand the significance of ideas contained in books by learning the historical and cultural context in which they were written.

Most of the individuals who need extra help in learning to read during elementary school are likely to be in the first stage of development of reading ability. They still need to learn to recognize words in print; that is, they still need to learn 1) responses to print, 2) use of their language and knowledge background when reading, and 3) integration of these major determinants of word recognition. Some of these students may also need to learn the language of print, such as the referents for a letter, word, sentence, or paragraph. Some may even have to learn the conventions of English print, such as scanning from left to right. Some junior high pupils might also have word recognition difficulties; if so, they are likely to have a limited word meaning vocabulary because they have not had sufficient reading experience to expand their vocabularies beyond those used in everyday language. They are also apt to have some difficulties in comprehension not only because they can't recognize some words or don't know their meaning, but also because they lack ability in integrating ideas, making inferences, and constructing the intended meaning of the passage. High school pupils who are low in reading ability are less likely to have word recognition difficulties but are more likely to have word meaning and knowledge limitations particularly when reading such subjects as science, mathematics, and social studies. Consequently, the teacher or tutor has to determine which components of reading ability need to be improved and then use the appropriate remedies.

Stress on word recognition. Teachers or tutors should know the principles of teaching word recognition and become acquainted with the various techniques for teaching individuals to identify printed words. Therefore, this section will emphasize principles, procedures, and strategies to employ in teaching word recognition.

Principles of Teaching Word Recognition

Proceed from the familiar to the unfamiliar a step at a time. Although there may be some disagreement, the following is an example of a sequence going from familiar to unfamiliar: Learning names for actual objects; associating a name with a picture of an object; recognizing a name in print in conjunction with a pictured object; and, finally, recognizing the printed word alone. In this sequence, one goes from a sensori-motor-perceptual type of experience to symbols to represent the experience. For example, from a name of a live dog to the name for a picture of a dog, to recognition of the printed word "dog" alone.

Focus attention on the printed stimuli. If students can identify a printed letter or word from a picture, they are not likely to look also at the print. Consequently, they will not learn to relate sounds to printed letters or words. To teach students to identify the letters of the alphabet, teach the features of the letters through a process of first *simultaneous* matching to print as shown in the illustration.

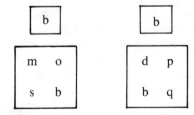

Examples of exercises for teaching simultaneous matching of letters. The teacher shows the student the top letter. Then the teacher has the student point to the identical letter below. On the left is an easy example; the example on the right is more difficult because the student has to compare and discriminate more features and maintain a left-to-right direction. The tall line comes first and the circle next. Then teach delayed matching to print. In delayed matching to print, the target letter is on one page and the choices are on the next page. This strategy forces students to remember the letter as a whole and compare it with each of the choices. In addition to learning to identify all the printed letters this way, students will have to learn the names of the letters and the sound to associate with each letter.

Although the English alphabet has only 26 letters and numbers from 1 to 9 (zero is a place holder), these letters and numbers appear in many different type fonts (e.g. bold face, italic, capital and small letters). Eventually, students have to learn to identify all of these type fonts; but in the beginning stage, they should have only one type font to learn. Indeed, teachers in the primary grades print letters in manuscript form when writing on the chalkboard or on students' papers.

Also, many letters have multiple sounds. For example, the letter *c* has the sound of *k* in *country* and s in *city*. Also, almost all letters have a silent sound in particular words. For example, *b* in *b*at is sounded, but *b* in lam*b* is silent. Also, some letters combine and require one sound for the combination, such as *ch*urch, *sh*oe, *th*is, bu*dge*.

Students eventually will have to learn *all* the sounds for each letter and when to switch from one sound to another. One strategy is to teach one sound for each letter and then alternate sounds. Another strategy is to teach multiple sounds simultaneously. Each strategy has its advantages and disadvantages. The sequence for teaching word recognition given in this manual is to teach the multiple sounds sequentially.

From dependence on the teacher to independence. To follow this principle, first tell students the whole word, then give hints, and finally let them figure out the word from the variety of techniques they may have learned. Thus, at first the teacher tells the pupils that the word is *dog*. Next time, the teacher gives individuals clues to help them figure out the word, such as inferring from the context (a picture context or a sentence context or both). For instance, "The _____ said, 'bow wow'." Or the direction to sound out the word, which implies that there is for the particular word a one-to-one sound symbol correspondence, may be considered. But this approach does not work for all words in the English language. For example, it works for *dog* but not for *right*. Therefore, the next principle is necessary.

Teach the individual a variety of ways of recognizing words. Each technique of word recognition breaks down or is inadequate because no one technique applies to all words in the English language. Skilled readers must learn to use a variety of techniques, and they must also learn to shift appropriately from one to another. For example, readers might use phonics to sound out *cat*. But in addition to sounding out *c-a-t*, readers must blend or put the sounds together to get the whole sound of *cat* which is then recognized as a familiar word. In contrast, individuals, except in a classroom, never hear anyone point to the actual object and say that's a *c-a-t* (usually pronounced cuh-ah-tuh).

Phonics or one-for-one sound symbol correspondences might work for *cat* but not for the word *right*. If individuals try to use phonics on *right*, it would come out *r-i-g-h-t*. No matter how many times the individual letters were sounded out, the word wouldn't come out *right*. To make the right word come out *right*, the individual would have to shift to another one of several techniques, such as using context plus the initial consonant to infer the word, as in the following sentence:

> After the boy answered the question, the teacher smiled and said, "That's r————."

Or students could have been taught the initial consonant *r* through such words as *r*ed, *r*ow, *r*un, and the phonogram, *ight* in such words as l*ight*, f*ight*, n*ight*. By substituting the initial consonant *r*, they would get the word *right*. Another way of recognizing the word is by using a combination of phonics and knowledge of silent letters, ri(gh)t. Students who have learned a variety of approaches can be flexible in recognizing words. If one approach doesn't work, they can switch to another. Learners are likely to do so not only if they know a variety of approaches but if they are also continuously testing their solution against the criterion of meaning or asking themselves, "Does this word pronounced this way make sense?"

Introduce new words and new techniques gradually and with adequate repetition so that the learner has a growing feeling of mastery. The basal readers or textbooks used in the primary grades for developing word recognition provide for about 10 repetitions of a newly introduced word and 5 repetitions of previously introduced words. It is estimated that the average individual requires about 38 repetitions to recognize a new word quickly and accurately.

Use an interesting way of having individuals practice recognizing new words. The most interesting way is to have individuals do a lot of reading in which they are likely to have to use the new words. The basal readers follow the introduction of new words with a story in which, by design, the new words appear several or more times. High interest, but low level difficulty reading material is likely to contain words that the teacher or tutor is trying to get the student to learn. At the end of this section are the following materials: a list of words that most pupils should know by the third grade and a list of high interest, low difficulty level books.

The word list was constructed by the late Edward Dolch who discovered that these words accounted for about 75 percent of all primary words and 50 percent of all adult words. The Dolch Readers and other materials published by Garrard Press systematically use this vocabulary (2).

The *Reader's Digest* Reading Skillbuilder is another set of high interest materials which start at a low level of difficulty and increase in difficulty (3). Together these two sets of materials would be very useful in teaching older individuals whose interests are more mature but for one reason or another have not learned how to read or how to read as well as they should.

Benefic Press publishes material such as *The Lost Uranium Mine*, which is also high interest, low level difficulty but introduces and uses new words cumulatively as in the basal reader strategy (4).

If you need to drill the individual on recognition of words, try to do so in a variety of ways. One technique that works well is to have individuals make up sentences using certain words. Write down the sentences and have the individuals read them. Then cut up the sentences into words and have them recognize the separate words. Then have the students group common initial consonants or common sounds in these words. Or they might group common syllables or prefixes and suffixes. Learners might also search through magazines for illustrations for their words. To help students create sentences for practicing new words, use the Singer Sentence Generator (5). The generator consists of four basic sentence forms:

1. *Noun*   *Verb*
   Abe   jumped.

2. *Noun*   *Verb*   *(Noun determiner)*   *(Adjective)*   *Noun*
   Debbie   saw   the   full   moon.

3. *Noun*   *Verb*   *Noun*   *(Noun determiner)*   *Noun*
   Woolfie   gave   Hallie   the   ball.

4. *Noun*   *Verb*   *Adjective*   *OR*   *Adverb*
   Ruth   is   pretty.
                 OR
   Ruth   works   quickly.

Students substitute words in the noun, verb, noun determiner, adjective, and adverb slots. To help students, new words and their corresponding slots may be color coded. Give students a 1 to 2 minute time limit to generate as many sentences as they can. Eventually, students will be able to generate sentences without the use of the sentence generators.

Knowledge of progress is extremely important. Two techniques that can be utilized for concretely showing progress are 1) make a file of new words and 2) construct a cumulative chart.

The card file might show the word in a sentence context on the front with the word in the corner divided into syllables and perhaps diacritically marked. On the back of the card, the word would appear in isolation. Individuals could test themselves by looking at the back of the card to see if they know the word in isolation and to see if they were right by reading the sentence and using its context clues to check. For young children, pictures might be used to identify the words (6).

The cumulative chart could be kept daily or weekly. Below are examples of these charts.

Daily: To indicate immediate consequence of practice in recognizing new words.

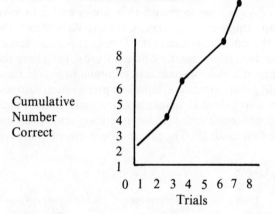

Weekly or monthly: To indicate cumulative number of new words learned.

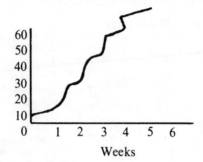

Cumulative
Number of New
Words

Weeks

In each lesson, try to maximize the probability of success.
Individuals who have experienced failure are extremely sensitive to
further failure. One strategy to attain success is to start by having
students tell a story. Or if students prefer, have them relate the activities
for the day or tell an anecdote. Copy down the story and teach the pupils
to read the story. First, go over the story and have individuals identify
words they don't recognize. Then, teach these words which will be put
into the word file and plotted on the chart. Afterward, have individuals
read the story. Next, cut up a copy of the story into sentences and have
individuals reassemble the sentences; then, cut the sentences into words.
Again, have the story reassembled. Finally, have individuals use the
words to make up new sentences.

From the very beginning, consult with the individuals'
classroom teacher. The tutor might get from the classroom teacher
valuable suggestions and even materials for helping the individual. In
any case, the tutor and the classroom teacher should be working
together to help the student. If the teacher or the student wants the tutor
to help with the daily assigned lesson, the tutor could use the above
principles with the assigned materials. Helping with the daily lesson is a
short range strategy that might pay off equally as well as a developmental, systematic program, provided the discrepancy between
students' assignment and level of reading ability is not so great that they
are overwhelmed by too many new words to learn. If so, tutors might
have to concentrate their efforts on the long range strategy of taking the
individuals back to a level where they can be successful and starting a
developmental reading program at that level.

For developmental or corrective reading instruction, it is
necessary to follow a sequence for teaching word recognition. There are
several logical sequences that could be used, but no one of them can be
said to be *the* sequence to follow. Below is one sequence.

A DEVELOPMENTAL SEQUENCE OF WORD RECOGNITION

Approximate Grade Level	
1	Sight words
1-2	Initial consonants
	Final consonants
	Consonant digraphs (ch, th)
	Consonant blends (*fry*, *sl*ed)
	Advanced consonant digraphs (*qu*een, si*nk,* dish*es,* si*ng*); variants (boy*s,* help*ed, go*ing)
	Silent consonants
	Contractions
	Simple structure of sentences and punctuation markers for speech patterns, such as use of commas, periods, question marks.
2	Vowels
	Long and short sounds
	Vowels in phonogram (right, make)
	Simple suffix (farm*er*)
	Rhyming endings
	More complex sentence structure and punctuation markers
3	Syllabication
4	Prefixes, suffixes, roots
5	Accent and dictionary work

Types of Word Recognition Techniques

The types of word recognition techniques can be grouped into three somewhat overlapping categories: predominantly visual clues, emphasis on meaning, and mainly analytical procedures.

Predominantly Visual Clues

Picture aids. Printed words are often learned by their association with pictures. For identifying nouns, pictures can be readily found in magazines. For other categories of speech, such as verbs and adjectives, cartoon strips can be used. A variety of ways of illustrating various parts of speech may be found in a small pocketbook, *English through Pictures* (7). This pocketbook may also be used for teaching English to bilingual children by having the children act out the sentences as they read them.

Sight words or instant recognition of words. Through recognition of the same words in a variety of situations, individuals build up a sight word repertoire. This repertoire increases as the individual matures in reading. Eventually, skilled readers recognize all words at sight or recognize them so rapidly that they become almost oblivious to the process because it occurs so quickly and so effortlessly. Two procedures are used for developing sight words:

- *Flash cards.* This procedure has already been discussed in the section on principles of teaching word recognition. It's a useful technique but should be used only for a short period of time because boredom sets in rapidly. However, there are a variety of techniques for making such exercises interesting, such as having the individual use the words to construct sentences.
- *Easy reading.* Seeing the same words in a variety of stories is the most interesting and best way of teaching sight word recognition. A list of interesting but easy to read books for older children is presented in the appendix. Guides to other high interest, low difficulty level material are listed in the references. These sources also include some comic books, which combine an abundance of picture aids and printed words.

Whether a book is easy to read depends on how well the reader can read. The rule of thumb is that if individuals have difficulty with more than one or two words per hundred, it's not an easy book for them. Whether a book is interesting, of course, depends upon the readers. For determining whether any book is easy, but interesting, the best procedure is to have individuals select their own books.

Emphasis on Meaning

Context clues. This technique consists of using a sentence to help the individual infer the meaning of the unknown word and then to think of the word itself. By looking at the initial consonant and other parts of the unknown word, the individual is employing a very powerful combination of word recognition techniques. The teaching procedure calls for constructing a sentence in which the unknown word is omitted. Then the individual reads the sentence and tries to infer the unknown word. These sentences may be placed on cards with the missing word on the back so that the flash card technique can be used and the cards then filed as tangible evidence of achievement. The tutor can teach the individual to recognize and use these clues whenever they appear in stories, and the tutor can also use this approach in giving hints for recognizing new words. Below are examples of various types of context clues (8).

- *Definition.* The unknown word is defined. "Tom liked to ride on the last car on the train. The last car on the train is the c _ _ _ _ _ _ _."
  (caboose)
- *Experience.* The individual can infer the word from experience. "Betty was going to grow her own flowers. In each row, she placed s _ _ _ _ ."
  (seeds)
- *Contrast.* The unknown word is opposite in meaning to known words or phrases. "She missed the noises of the big city. On the farm it was very q _ _ _ _ ."
  (quiet)
- *Familiar expression.* The unknown word is part of an idiom of everyday expression. "To his surprise, the big man was as g _ _ _ _ _ as a lamb."
  (gentle)
- *Summary.* The unknown word sums up the ideas in the preceding sentences. "First, Tom saw the riders rope the steers. Then he laughed at the cowboy clown on his horse. Then he watched the cowboys race around the ring. Tom had a lot of fun at the r _ _ _ _ ."
  (rodeo)
- *Reflection of a mood or situation.* The unknown word explains mood of the story. "After a few days away from home at camp, she began to miss her family, her dog, and her friends. She was h_ _ _ _ _ _ _ ."
  (homesick)

Compound words. Words which represent the combination of two words may be recognized when separated and the meaning of the two words gives the meaning of the combined word. At the primary grade level, such words as *summertime* and *firefighter* can be recognized this way. One technique is to have each part of the compound word on a separate card and bring the two cards together so they appear to make one word. Or the two parts of the word can be underlined separately, e.g., fire fighter. At advanced grade levels, another technique may be used. For example, the word *optometrist* may be drawn up from the component parts:

optical	water meter	cyclist
optic nerve	thermometer	pharmacist
	speedometer	psychologist

Each of these words also may be presented in the context of a sentence. After this presentation, the individual could put together the component parts to recognize and understand the meaning of optometrist. This technique is technically referred to as morphological analysis, breaking a word down into its meaning components of prefix, root word, and suffix. A list of frequent morphological components can be found in the appendix, and the references indicate sources for additional lists.

Analytical Techniques

Structural and phonetic analysis are the two major types of analytical techniques.

Structural analysis is synonymous with morphological analysis. Included in structural analysis are the following:

- Compound and hyphenated words (cement-mixer).
- Root words and their variants which include the various endings to indicate tense and number, such as *rush/rushed* and *boy/boys*.
- Syllabication, the parts of a word which may or may not represent meaning components, such as prefixes or suffixes, but do represent boundaries between sequences of sounds in a word.

Since morphological analysis was discussed above, structural analysis in this section will emphasize syllabication. In general, a word has as many syllables as heard vowel sounds. To teach syllabication, do the following:

- Pupil and teacher should first pronounce the word carefully.
- Identify the number of heard vowel sounds.
- Group together about five words that fit a principle of syllabication. Teach pupils to divide each word into its syllables. Have pupils try to formulate the rule. Then have pupils supply or search for words that fit the rule. After they have learned the rules presented below, they can classify new words according to the rules. Most important is to have pupils use syllabication as a technique for recognizing new words.

Rules for Syllabication

1. If there is only one heard vowel sound in a word, the word is monosyllabic and, therefore, cannot be further divided. Examples: *late, night, trees.*

2. In words containing two heard vowel sounds, if two consonants are together in the word with vowels on either side, the word is usually divided between the consonants. Examples: *af ter, but ter, bar gain.*
3. Affixes (prefixes and suffixes) usually form a separate syllable. Examples: *un*happy, live*ly*. (Note: *ed* is usually only a separate syllable when preceded by *t* or *d* as in *wanted* and *needed.* When preceded by other consonants, *ed* does not form a separate syllable as in *called, rushed, liked.*)
4. If there is one consonant between two vowels in a two-syllable word and the first vowel sound is long, the long vowel usually ends the first syllable and the consonant begins the second syllable. Examples: *la dies, po lite.* (The first syllable is called an "open" syllable.)
5. If there is one consonant between two vowels in a two-syllable word and the first vowel is short, the consonant usually ends the first syllable and the second vowel sound begins the second syllable. Examples: *cam el, mer ry.* (First syllable is called a "closed" syllable.)
6. Compound words are divided into their component parts. Examples: *high way, rail road, snow flake.*
7. *Le* endings are special cases. If the word ends in *ck* when *le* is taken off, then *le* is a separate syllable. Examples: crack*le*, pick*le*. In all other words, *le* takes the preceding consonant. Examples: ea*gle*, can*dle*.
8. For words which contain more than two syllables, follow the above principles, proceeding from the largest to the smallest division of the word.
   - Inspect for compound word. Examples: *steel worker, kinder garten.*
   - Take off affix. Work*er*, kind*er* garten.
   - If one or more of the parts has more than one heard vowel.
   - Inspect for special "le" endings.

Structural analysis, one of the two major types of analytical techniques, has been explained above. Phonics will now be explained.

Phonics. "Sounding out" words, or applying phonetic principles to the recognition of new words, is useful for about 80 to 85 percent of words. One procedure for applying phonics or relating sounds to letters (phoneme-grapheme correspondences) is the following:
   - Group known sight words with a common consonant or vowel. For example: can   cut   car.
   - Have individuals read each word to make sure each word is a known sight word.

         Singer

- Have pupils notice the initial letters of the words are alike and the initial sounds are alike. Tell the pupils the name of the letter (small and capital letter).
- To test whether pupils have learned the sound for the initial consonant, have them give additional words with the same initial sound. If they give the following words, form them into two columns.

cold	kite	city
cup	kit	cent
cap	kind	

- In the above examples, point out that some words have the same phoneme-grapheme correspondence; some words have the same sound, but a different letter; and some words have the same grapheme or letter and different phoneme. This discovery will help pupils limit their generalizations and perhaps help them become flexible in shifting from one phoneme-grapheme correspondence to another in recognizing words.
- Pupils can also learn phonograms the same way.

came	*night*
game	*right*
tame	*light*

After reading through the list of words with a common phonogram, have pupils supply or search for additional words with the same phonogram. (See list of references for sets of phonograms.)

- With knowledge of consonants and phonograms, pupils can figure out new words by means of consonant substitution. For example, pupils who know *tell* and *sell* and initial consonant *b* can then figure out the new word *bell*.
- Although pupils can and do learn to read by implicitly using rules, it may help to know the rules. To teach them, proceed in the following way. Teach inductively by presenting words that illustrate a vowel principle and having words categorized under that principle. The following vowel and consonant rules, except when indicated, have a 75 percent utility rating. That is, they are applicable to words likely to occur in the elementary grades. (However, rules are helpful if they apply to a large number of words, have a relatively small percentage of exceptions, and help students identify novel words. Not many

rules fit these criteria. See Theodore Clymer and related critiques by Thomas C. Barrett and Nicholas J. Silvaroli on "The Utility of Phonic Generalizations in the Primary Grades." In L.M. Gentile, M.L. Kamil, and J.S. Blanchard (Eds.), *Reading Research Revisited.* Columbus, Ohio: Merrill, 1983. Only 18 out of 45 rules or generalizations had 75 percent or more utility for words taken from four series of basal readers and from I. Lorge and E. Thorndike's *The Teachers' Wordbook of 30,000 Words.*)

Vowel Rules
1. Long vowel sounds are usually the names of the vowel letters, āte, īde, ōpen, ūse or the following group of words: Ā sweēt, nīce, ōld, ūnicorn.
2. When two vowels are together in a word, the first is usually long and the second is usually silent. This principle has only a 45 percent utility rating. Examples: āid, ēast, trīed, bōat, rūeful.
3. A more specific form of rule (2) is that when the five vowels are *ee,* they have the long e sound. For example, *seem.* However, this rule has a 75 percent utility rating.
4. But there are many exceptions to the above rule, particularly when the first vowel is followed by *u, o,* and *i.* Examples: haul, caught, good, spoon, broom, said, oil.
5. In words containing two vowels, one of which is final *e,* the final *e* is usually silent and the preceding vowel is usually long. Example: ate, eve, ice, use. This principle has a 63 percent utility rating.
6. In monosyllabic words containing one *e* and ending in a consonant, the *e* is usually short. Example: pet.
7. Single vowels followed by *l, r,* or *w* usually have a blend sound. Examples: talk, ball, car, far, saw, raw.
8. When *y* ends a monosyllabic word it has a vowel sound. If there are no other vowels in the word, it has the sound of long *i.* Examples: my, try. If *a* precedes *y,* then *a* is long and *y* is silent. If *y* ends a two syllable word, it frequently has the sound of long e. Examples: merry, scary, surely. If *y* is preceded by another vowel, there is a different sound for both. Examples: they, boy.

Consonant Rules
1. Consonants are sometimes silent or not sounded. Examples: lam*b,* nigh*t,* *gh*ost, *h*our, *m*nemonic, *k*now, *p*neumonia, i*s*land, *w*rote. These silent consonants must be learned as sight words. That is, a reader has to learn that in certain words, there is one or more

consonants that are silent. This is frequently true for words beginning with *kn* (know, knife), words that have *gh* in them (light, night, right) and words ending in *mb* (lamb, thumb, limb). Although silent consonants make phonics inapplicable to many words, silent consonants are important for word recognition, particularly for discriminating homonyms (words sounded alike, but spelled differently), such as buy/by, two/to, know/no. If words did not contain silent letters, we would have to use some other clues, such as diacritical markings for determining pronunciation. For example, try to read this sentence in which the silent letters have been omitted:

We caut eit fishes at eit this morning and at them at nit.

The same sentence with the silent letters in reads: We caught eight fishes at eight this morning and ate them at night.

2. The combination of *ch* in a monosyllabic word makes only one sound. Example: *teach.* Exception: *machine.*
3. When *c* is followed by *a* or *o*, the *c* has the sound of *k*. Examples: *cat, cot.* But when *c* is followed by *e* or *i,* it usually has the sound of *s*. Examples: *cell, city.*
4. In monosyllabic words with the consonants *ght* together, *gh* are silent. Example: *eight.*
5. In disyllabic words with twin consonants, the first consonant is heard and the second is usually silent. Example: *merry.*
6. When a word ends in *ck*, it usually has the sound of *k*. Example: pi*ck.*
7. When *the, sh,* or *ch* is preceded by a vowel in disyllabic words the digraph remains and goes with either the first or second syllable. Examples: *wishes, dashes.*

Cautions in Teaching Word Recognition

Proceed only as rapidly as pupils can be cumulatively successful. Whether teaching new sight words, a new structural analysis technique, or a new phonic principle, provide sufficient practice and use of the new instruction in various reading situations so that pupils do not get overloaded with too much too quickly. Some pupils need a slow rate of learning, and others can have a faster rate of learning. Sometimes the same pupil can learn some things slowly and others quickly. You have to judge what is the best pace or rate of learning for your pupils. Begin each session with a review of the instruction at the previous session, and after pupils demonstrate they remember what was taught previously, then go on to new instruction. If pupils do not remember, then have a quick review of the previous instruction before going on to new instruction. Then be sure to evaluate your rate of instruction to determine whether it fits your pupils' rate of learning. If you can, keep a graph or chart of the rate of instruction.

Plan each lesson carefully. Make sure you know what you want your pupils to accomplish at each session. At least make an outline of the lesson. A typical lesson might include the following:

- Review words.
- Introduce new words (print word in sentence) and discuss them to get pronunciation, ways of recognizing word, word meaning, and similarity (pronunciation, common word recognition elements, or similar or opposite meaning) to previous words, and experiences associated with the word.
- Have pupils recognize new word in a variety of sentences.
- Make a card for card file for each new word.
- Make experience chart using the new words or read story containing words.
- Teach the student to be an active reader. Try to arouse curiosity for reading the story by having pupil formulate questions about the story from knowing its title or from looking at the illustrations. If the story is in material that has questions at the end, let pupils read questions first. Then read the story. Later let them predict in advance what the questions are when they read the title of the story. The eventual objective is to get the pupils to formulate questions during reading and thus read to answer these questions. This process will make them active readers.
- Have pupils re-read story into tape recorder and then listen to playback. Let pupils evaluate their own performance.
- Teach new word recognition skill and have pupil practice the skill in an interesting way.

Try to work with pupils at least twice a week. At first, do not require pupils to do anything outside of the teaching or tutoring session. As pupils become successful they will ask to take books home or will begin to bring books, new words, or materials to the session. Gradually, you might begin to assign homework. Be sure, though, that pupils know how to do the homework. If they are to read a book at home, all the words in the book should be known. As new words are recognized, pupils should be given books in which they come across words that can be figured out from what was already learned in the tutoring session.

As much as possible, plan and evaluate with your pupils. Find out what your pupils think their difficulty is, how they are trying to solve it, how students try to read, and what they would like to learn. Make the process of teaching and learning a mutual situation with you and your pupils working together to achieve a common goal.

Work together developing automaticity in word recognition. Automaticity lies beyond accuracy in word recognition. A highly experienced automobile driver is oblivious to the mechanics of starting a car, shifting, and stopping and, consequently, can concentrate attention on the conditions of the road, other cars, and directions to reach a destination. Similarly, the automatic reader only minimally attends to word recognition and maximally concentrates on thinking about the content. Readers develop this automaticity by reading lots of relatively easy material. They frequently read many books on their own during their elementary school years. Many read series books, such as *Tom Swift, Nancy Drew, Rover Boys, Sue Barton, Dr. Dolittle, and Adventures of Tarzan.* Help your students develop automaticity cumulatively by reading many books that have familiar plots and very few new words but nevertheless are interesting to the students. In short, follow a stepwise procedure: teach some new words and then have students practice using the words by generating sentences containing the words and by reading a lot of materials that contain these words until the students automatically recognize the words. Then take them on to a new set of words or a new word identification technique. This principle applies to any aspect of reading instruction. A schematic of this procedure follows (*9*).

Use the method of repeated reading for acquisition of comprehension. Students who have difficulty in reading often struggle with word identification so much that they may not get to comprehend a passage before they have to go on to another lesson on another passage and repeat the struggle. A similar experience occurs to all readers when trying to read in a foreign language. They go through a page trying to identify the words and think of the meaning of each word. When they reach the bottom of the page, they can't remember what they read at the top of the page. They have to go back and reread. After several readings of the same page, they may finally comprehend it. Beginning and poor readers have the same experience when reading in their own language. To help them, have them read and re-read the same passage, first to identify the printed words and next to discuss and understand each paragraph. Finally, have them read the entire passage and find answers to questions the teacher poses and eventually questions that they, themselves, have formulated. Variants of this procedure also may be used. For example, the teacher could tape a story. Students could listen

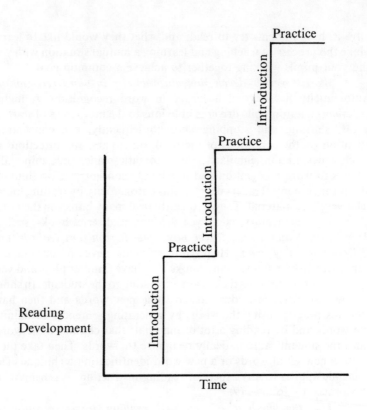

to the tape of the whole story and then listen and read along with a paragraph or a page at a time. Eventually, students should be able to read the entire story alone and comprehend it. Of course, start with very short stories and progress to longer ones, as students become cumulatively successful (*10, 11*).

Teach students to read and learn from texts in each content area. Each content area has its own technical vocabulary, symbols, information, and explanations. Students can be good readers in one content area because they have the necessary vocabulary, symbols, background knowledge, and are familiar with the explanation and modes of reasoning used in that area, but they may be poor readers in the content area where their resources are less than adequate.

In short, readers have a profile of reading abilities in the various content areas that reflect their backgrounds, interests, and curricular experiences, in and out of school. Those who also have pursued a

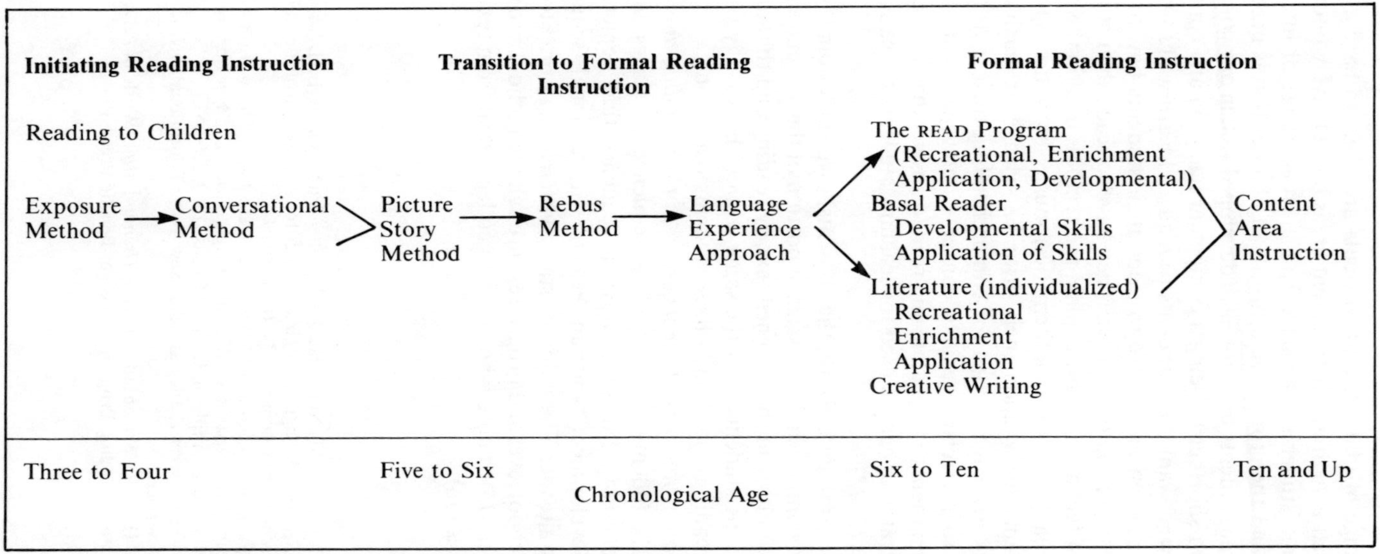
Initiating Reading Instruction
Transition to Formal Reading Instruction
Formal Reading Instruction
Reading to Children
Exposure Method
Conversational Method
Picture Story Method
Rebus Method
Language Experience Approach
The READ Program
(Recreational, Enrichment
Application, Developmental)
Basal Reader
Developmental Skills
Application of Skills
Literature (individualized)
Recreational
Enrichment
Application
Creative Writing
Content Area Instruction
Three to Four
Five to Six
Six to Ten
Ten and Up
Chronological Age

Figure 1. Time line for sequence of reading instruction.

narrow range of interests and curricula are likely to have a profile of abilities that is high in a few content areas but relatively poor in other areas. Some students may have had a broad range of interests and curricula and therefore have a profile of abilities that is high in many areas. Some students may not have developed well in any content area. There is no shortcut to being a competent reader in any content area. Teachers who want their students to read and learn well from texts in their own content areas have to teach their students how to read and learn from the texts they select. They have to teach their students the meaning of technical terms; explain the symbols used in the particular content area (chemistry, mathematics, music, literature, sports); and have students draw upon their prior knowledge or teach them the necessary knowledge needed for comprehending their texts and show them how to interrelate the facts, concepts, and generalizations in their texts. Teach them to formulate and read to answer their own questions. Various strategies can be used for teaching students to read and learn from text (*12, 13*).

One strategy is to use the students' own classroom text. Teach students to comprehend the assigned portion of the text and show them how you would read the assigned text by reading and thinking aloud. Then have the students read the same section. Eventually you can do alternate readings and finally have students read alone.

Know what stage students are at in their reading development. In general, students go through a sequence of stages in reading development (*14*). Figure 1 shows a sequence that depicts normal reading development and an eclectic instructional sequence for developing a reader. The sequence starts with reading stories to children at the preschool level and progresses through high school and into each content area (*15*). Those who go on to college learn from texts at even higher levels (*16*).

References
1. Singer, H. "IQ Is and Is Not Related to Reading," in S. Wanat (Ed.), *Issues in Evaluating Reading.* Arlington, Virginia: Center for Applied Linguistics, 1977. Also in Eric Document Resumes, 1974. (ED 088 004)
2. *Basic Sight Words.* Champaign, Illinois: Garrard Press. This word list also can be found in M.A. Tinker & C.M. McCullough, *Teaching Elementary Reading* (2nd ed.). New York: Appleton-Century-Crofts, 1962, 550-557.
3. *Reader's Digest Service.* Pleasantville, New York: Educational Division, Reader's Digest Services.
4. Bamman, H., & R. Whitehead. *The Lost Uranium Mine.* World of Adventure Supplementary Reading Program. Chicago: Benefic Press, 1964.

5. Singer, H., & S. Beasley. "Motivating a Disabled Reader," in M. Douglass (Ed.), Thirty-Seventh Yearbook of Claremont College Reading Conference. Claremont, California: Claremont Graduate School, 1970.
6. Garrard Press' "Popper Words" are based on this principle.
7. Richards, I.A., & C.M. Gibson. *English through Pictures.* Pocketbooks, 1953.
8. McCullough, C.M. "The Recognition of Context Clues in Reading," *Elementary English Review,* 1945, *22,* 1-5.
9. Samuels, S. Jay, & D. LaBerge and related articles by L. Melton & W. Otto. "A Theory of Automaticity in Reading. Looking Back: A Retrospective Analysis of the LaBerge-Samuels Reading Model," in L. Gentile, M. Kamil, & J. Blanchard (Eds.), *Reading Research Revisited.* Columbus, Ohio: Merrill, 1983.
10. Samuels, S. Jay. "The Method of Repeated Reading," *Reading Teacher,* 1979, *32,* 403-408.
11. Chomsky, C. "After Decoding: What?" *Language Arts,* 1976, *53,* 288-297.
12. Herber, H. *Teaching Reading in Content Areas* (2nd ed.). Englewood Cliffs, New Jersey: Prentice-Hall, 1978.
13. Singer, H., & D. Donlan. *Reading and Learning from Text.* Boston: Little, Brown, 1980.
14. Chall, J.S. *Stages of Reading Development.* New York: McGraw-Hill, 1983.
15. Tzeng, O.J.L., & H. Singer (Eds.). *Perception of Print.* Hillsdale, New Jersey: Erlbaum, 1981.
16. Singer, H., & T. Bean (Eds.). *Learning from Text Project for 1981-1982: Conceptualization, Prediction, and Intervention.* Riverside, California: University of California Learning from Text Project, 1982. (ED 223 989)

Chapter 6
TEACHING COMPREHENSION SKILLS

David L. Shepherd
Hofstra University

The reader's competency in word recognition and study techniques leads toward the main purpose for reading which is to comprehend the information and ideas expressed on the printed page. Unless there is comprehension—understanding—the reader will get neither pleasure nor information. Therefore, this chapter deals with the major comprehension skills and methods and materials for the effective teaching of them.

Comprehension in reading is the same as the comprehension of language. Orally, a listener attempts to understand what is being said; graphically, the reader attempts to understand what is written. In both instances, the individual is involved with language. As soon as one begins to represent speech sounds with graphic symbols, one begins to read. Graphic symbols are the letters of the alphabet in various combinations to form words. When reading, individuals should realize they are working symbolically with their native language—the one they speak. Reading is basically talk written down.

Comprehension, whether in listening to oral speech or reading a written form of it, is dependent upon the student's basic background of knowledge and experience. One of the first concerns in teaching comprehension skills is to ascertain the individual's scope of knowledge with the intent to fill in the gaps where necessary. Tutors need to do many things. They need to find out the nature of their students' backgrounds and add to students' experiences by using audiovisual media, by providing actual experiences, and by fostering wide reading of a variety of printed materials.

In teaching individuals to read with understanding, one has a twofold purpose. The most immediate purpose is to use reading for *satisfying the practical needs of living.* The wish is to help students maintain themselves in society—to get and hold a job and to use the common reference materials of everyday life. The other purpose, and the long range one, is to help students *use reading as a pleasurable activity.* It enables students to use books, magazines, and newspapers and thereby have access to the world of ideas. With both purposes, tutors will strive to have individuals become knowledgeable as well as learn to appreciate, evaluate, and apply information.

Basic Skills of Comprehension

The effective reader uses a number of skills to comprehend the information found in printed materials. The skills also help in organizing the various items of information so the interrelationships are apparent. The skills of comprehension follow.

1. *Recognizing the main idea.* This skill involves readers in getting to the nucleus or core of the information. Usually, the readers give the main idea when they say, "The story is about _____." Each paragraph has a main idea which may be stated directly in the paragraph.

2. *Noting details.* This skill of comprehension is considered to be one of the easiest. It is noting and understanding the factual data. Details relate to a main idea by adding some type of factual information about it. They may explain, illustrate, define, or describe the main idea. Though details are not in themselves difficult, readers will need to group them around each appropriate main idea.

3. *Organizing ideas.* The ability to use this skill means that readers are able to see interrelationships among the ideas in a reading selection. It often involves grouping the ideas in accordance with some criteria such as, likenesses, differences, for and against, steps of an argument, and items of description.

4. *Seeing the sequence of ideas.* Actually, this skill is also a way to organize ideas. Seeing sequence means that readers are able to relate in proper order, usually from beginning to the end, the various steps of a process or events in a story.

5. *Following directions.* This is a very useful and practical skill in which readers must proceed slowly step by step in a definite sequence to carry out some project.

6. *Evaluating information.* Readers judge the accuracy and logic of the information. This is a step beyond the basic skills of understanding what an author has written. Readers question and judge the author's ideas and intent.
7. *Predicting and anticipating what will happen.* When readers are able to predict and anticipate, they are comprehending basically and trying to outguess the author. To predict or anticipate what an author may write means that the reader is thinking with the author.
8. *Using the information.* The reader's ability to use the information contained in a reading selection is the final goal of comprehension. Sometimes the use is direct, such as in following directions; at other times, the use is subtle and involves a possible change in the reader's attitudes or beliefs.

Prerequisites to Effective Comprehension

Knowing and applying a skill are not enough. There are other conditions which help to bring about good comprehension:

1. *Establish purpose for reading.* This is a basic, simple requirement which many times is overlooked. Readers should look for some specific information during reading. They should have some questions in mind. Knowing why one reads will tend to keep attention focused on the content of the material; to indicate a direction toward the information to be acquired; and to help determine if the reading should be fast or slow, intensive or casual.
2. *Know how to locate information.* Readers must know how to find information in everyday reference sources. In current society, such reference materials include the following: air, bus, and train schedules; automobile driver's manuals; telephone directories; television, radio, and movie programs; mail order catalogs; recipes in cookbooks; operator's manuals for the handling of some types of machinery; and directions in a line of work. These are just a few of the everday practical references which most persons are required to use. These references furnish excellent study materials for those individuals who are attempting to improve in reading.
3. *Knowing the meaning of words.* The scope of readers' vocabularies is dependent upon the breadth and depth of their backgrounds of experience and information. Much

audiovisual material may need to be used in order to increase readers' experiential backgound for vocabulary understanding.

When teaching vocabulary, the teacher may begin with practical words such as those found in the common references cited and other words used by people in their everyday living. Words found on street signs, in stores, and in restaurants and other public buildings may be used in the beginning.

The way the words are used in a sentence or paragraph may be helpful, although an individual's background will determine the usefulness of the technique. Readers also need to be alerted to the meaning of a word when it is defined by the author. Operators' manuals often will define new technical terms as they are used.

Instruction in the use of glossaries and dictionaries, obviously, is in order.

Finally, the classification of ideas—the organization of thought—can be helpful both as a means to increase meaning as well as to bring about a greater clarity of thought. For instance, have individuals see what words could be listed under such topic words as trees, birds, furniture, buildings and metals.

4. *Determine the organization of the information.* As we have just noted, a beginning can be made toward informational organization by the use of words which classify the information. The reader should be able to see how an author has arranged and related ideas. Individual facts are usually not significant by themselves and are likely to be easily forgotten; whereas, a logical grouping of facts suggests a structure of information indicating how the facts are related. Two techniques a reader can use are to note the pattern of the writing and to be aware of words, sometimes called signal or clue words, that indicate the relationship of the ideas. Some common patterns of writing are a main idea with supporting details, an order of information such as found in a sequence or a chronology, the step-by-step progression of a process, and a definition with explanation and/or illustration. Within these patterns, signal words can indicate the inherent relationship or the direction of thought. Such words as *and, also, besides, furthermore,* and *in addition* indicate that new but related information is coming. Such words as *but,*

whereas, and *however* indicate an alteration or a condition upon an idea.

5. *Relate the material to be read to readers' backgrounds of experience.* This coordinating will not be difficult with practical materials since they relate to the usual tasks of living. Interest is developed and understanding is enhanced as individuals are able to relate the content of their reading to past experiences or previous knowledge.

Suggestions for Teaching Comprehension

These suggestions will center around two major areas. The first is the skill of asking questions appropriate to the skill to be taught. The second will be specific classroom suggestions for teaching the skills of comprehension.

Questions for Skill Development

A prerequisite to the effective teaching of comprehension skills is the ability to ask questions which require the use of each specific skill as it is being taught and practiced. Suggested questions are listed below for each major comprehension skill.

1. *Purpose questions to keep in mind while reading.*
   - Would you have made the same decision as _____?
   - Can you find out if _____?
   - What is the main idea of the author?
   - What is the viewpoint of the author?
   - What are the steps of the process?
2. *Asking for the main idea.*
   - What is the topic sentence (main idea) of this paragraph?
   - What is the main point(s) of the author?
   - What would be a good headline for this paragraph?
   - What would be a good title for this article or story?
   - What is the main idea?
3. *Noting details.*
   - What facts did the author give?
   - What time does _____?
   - How much liquid _____?
   - Where did the event happen?
   - When did the main character get home?
4. *Seeing the organization of ideas.*
   - In what ways are the two alike? Different?

- List the arguments for _____ .
- List the various methods of land conservation.
5. *Understanding sequence* (following directions).
    - What steps do we follow when _____ ?
    - What happened first _____ ?
    - What do we do after _____ ?
6. *Evaluating information.*
    - Is the information biased?
    - Is the author qualified to write about the subject?
    - What is the author's intent?
    - Does the author use factual or emotional language?
7. *Predicting and anticipating.*
    - What do you think will happen next?
    - Since he lost the fight, what will he do?
    - What do you think will be the result of _____ ?
8. *Using the information.*
    - What principle law, or phenomenon, is cited or explained?
    - Does the author give the reader any clues of how the information can be used? If so, what are the clues?
    - Explain why you think the information may be for background only and not for an immediate use.
    - Determine if the implementation is concrete (i.e., how something is to be done) or suggests a change of attitude in point-of-view or possibly is just additional information that has no immediate use.

Suggested Classroom Activities for Teaching the Skills of Comprehension

1. *Recognizing the main idea.*
    Have students express the main idea in their own words.
    Underline the main ideas in several paragraphs in a textbook and note where they are usually found.
    Write a paragraph giving a main idea.
    Give titles to paragraphs.
    State an appropriate headline for a selection for a paragraph.
    Practice using headings in heavy black print.
    Check the main idea with the introductory and summary paragraphs of a chapter.
    Select from a list of sentences the one that best expresses the main idea of a paragraph of a selection.

2. *Noting details.*

Note relative importance of details by such signal words as *above all, most important, of greatest value.*

Notice the ways in which the author indicates the relative importance of details: a) by giving more space to one fact than to another, b) by the use of introductory remarks such as *above all* or *most important,* c)by organization as indicated by heading in heavy black print, d) by the use of italics, e) by picture and other graphic aids, and f) by the list of important words at the end of a chapter.

Select a character you like or dislike and determine what the author has done to make you react to the character.

Match a series of details with a list of main ideas.

Study the regulations for operating a piece of equipment.

Answer questions of detail included in a selection.

3. *Organizing ideas.*

Classify objects in a room according to their function.

Tell what items belong in classifications, such as food and recreation.

Study the table of contents to note the organization of a book.

Categorize information (ways of travel, ways to communicate, etc.).

4. *Seeing the sequence.*

Read the main ideas in a chapter to get an overview in sequence of the material covered.

Enumerate the steps of a process or in a chain of historical events.

Notice the words that suggest the introduction of another step, such as *then, finally, another, subsequently.*

Note the steps in proper order for constructing some object, doing some written assignment, doing an experiment.

List the chain of events leading to some scientific discovery.

5. *Evaluating information.*

Note when the material was written.

Analyze the information and evolve what you think the author's intent or purpose is.

Classify the words the author uses in two columns: factual words, emotional words.

Find out the author's background in the subject.

Rewrite material in which you present the information but also give a definite positive or negative point of view.

6. *Predicting and anticipating.*

In a situation of confusion and indecision, have readers anticipate what they think will happen next.

Why?

Shepherd

Compare present day conditions with those of a certain period in the past; decide what will likely happen next.

Consider what will happen next in light of a) background events, b) characters involved, and c) the situation.

Make up endings for stories.

Estimate the answer to an arithmetic problem.

7. *Using the information.*

State the principle, law, or phenomenon the author is discussing.

Note how the information can be used.

The comprehension skills are basic to a reader's practical as well as pleasurable use of reading. These are the skills which give purpose to the reading act. It is in the comprehension area that reading becomes thinking with the author through the medium of the printed page.

Examples of Paragraphs and Questions to Foster Specific Skill Development

1. *Recognizing the main idea.*

Drivers of cars should become familiar with the signs of failing brakes since good brakes are important for safety in driving. After a car has been used for some time, brakes become worn and the linings must be replaced. Oil and grease may leak into the brakes and make them slip if the wrong kind of grease has been put in the rear axle. Water may get in from driving in wet, stormy weather through puddles and flooded roads so that the brakes will not hold properly. Dirt from dry and dusty roads may filter into the drum and make the brakes "grab." Also, an unusual amount of driving in hilly country may warp the brake drums, reducing braking power.

a. What is the topic sentence of this paragraph? Where is it found?

b. What would be a good headline for this paragraph?

c. Where would you find some more information about this topic?

2. *Noting details.*

Simple and consistent maintenance will keep venetian blinds looking like new. They should be cleaned frequently with a soft brush. The cleaning also can be done with a vacuum cleaner. At times, the pulleys should be oiled at the top of the blind with a drop of oil. Remember to handle the blinds gently. Do not raise or lower them with great force. If the window is open on a windy day, raise the blinds all the way to the top so they do not clatter in the breeze.

a. What suggestions are given for cleaning venetian blinds?

b. How should venetian blinds be handled?

    c. How do you keep the blinds from clattering in the breeze?

    d. How can you take care of the pulleys?

3. *Organizing ideas.*

Screw extractors are used to remove broken screws. There are several types of extractors; each is supplied in sets with sizes for screws of varying diameters. Perhaps the most commonly used type is the Ezy-Out which is tapered and has a coarse spiral, resembling a thread, with very sharp ridges. The sharp ridges on the extractor "bite" into the sides of the hole in the broken stud or screw so it can be screwed out. Another type of tapered extractor is made with four straight flutes which have sharp edges. This tool is tapped into the drilled hole with a hammer to force the sharp edges of the flutes into the sides of the hole and grip the broken stud so it can be unscrewed. A third type is perfectly straight without any taper and has three sharp splines. The extractor is driven into the hole with a hammer. It then gets sufficient grip on the broken stud to permit screwing it out.

    a. List the types of screw extractors.

    b. What words signal the description of each type of screw extractor?

    c. In what way is each of the screw extractors alike?

4. *Seeing the sequence of ideas.*

The events leading up to the establishment of the national government covered a span of a half century or more. For many years around the mid-seventeenth century, the colonists of North America had trouble with the French and with Indians. This conflict was known as the French and Indian War. Finally, the French and Indians were defeated and England gained Canada and all the land between the Appalachian Mountains and the Mississippi River. At that time, England started to tax the colonies. A quarrel developed between England and the thirteen colonies because the colonies refused to pay the taxes. In fact, the colonies declared their independence from England in 1776. This quarrel resulted in the Revolutionary War. The colonies finally won their independence from England in 1781. The new states were still in difficulty, however, because there was not a strong central government. Under the Articles of Confederation, conditions became very difficult and confused. Therefore, the Constitutional Convention was called and met in Philadelphia in 1787. The present constitution, which determines the structure of the present national government, was written at this convention. Under the new constitution, George Washington became the first president in 1789.

a. List the events leading up to the formation of the federal government.
b. Which happened first, the declaration of independence or the winning of independence?
c. What was the first war mentioned in this paragraph? The last war?
5. *Following directions.*

      Additional water fixtures in a house require the installation of new lengths of pipe. Such additional plumbing requires detailed planning for the new plumbing branches. The general procedure for new installations follows several steps. First, study the plumbing system of the house to find the best place to "hook on" the new pipe line to the existing water supply pipe. Connecting the new line to a distribution pipe near to the water meter is usually a good place because adequate water pressure is assured. Second, shut off the water supply for the whole house. Third, look for an elbow or straight coupling closest to the point where the new line is to be joined to the existing distribution pipe. Fourth, substitute a tee fitting at this point and connect the first length of new pipe to fit it. Fifth, continue the lengths of new pipe away from this junction. And sixth, secure the pipe to structural beams of the house by means of straps placed about ten inches apart.
a. What is the third step in adding additional water fixtures?
b. Where is the best location usually for the new pipe line to be "hooked on"?
c. How far apart are the straps placed?
d. How many steps are mentioned in this operation?
6. *Evaluating information.*

      Conservation is a great concern to human beings today, especially with continued increases in the world population. Conservation means the production and wise use of our natural resources, such as the soil, water, forests, minerals, wildlife and human resources. The earth may seem large to us, but it is finite. The resources are limited; there is a certain amount and then no more. However, some resources are renewable. Forest, wildlife, and human resources are renewable. Soil, water, and minerals are not. Conservationists who study ways we can use resources wisely maintain that our well being is dependent upon a wise use of both renewable and nonrenewable resources. It should be everybody's business.
a. What reaction to the information does the author wish the reader to have?

b. What kind of language is used—factual or emotional?

c. What further information would be helpful to the reader?

d. Explain whether you think the author's consideration, expressed in the last sentence, is logical.

7. *Predicting and anticipating.*

Judging Your Occupational Choice

Once you have determined your occupational goal, you need to relate it to a specific occupational choice. There may be several occupations which would satisfy the goal you have set for yourself. Therefore, here are three guides you can use to decide on the specific job you wish. The first guide is your satisfaction with the job. You should analyze how happy you would be with the work, if you can do it well, and if you can get recognition and advancement. Investigate also the working conditions and the friendliness of the people. The second guide is income. Note the average income you can expect and determine if this will be adequate for you. Note if there are opportunities for earning extra income. The third guide is the opportunity you will have in the work. Determine if the work is in an expanding field or in one which will shortly become old-fashioned. Look at the competition from others and determine how you compare. Adequate consideration given to these three guides will do much to guarantee success and satisfaction in your vocational choice.

a. Read the title and jot down how you would judge your occupational choice. Then read the paragraph and note how you agree or disagree with the author.

b. What other guides would you list?

c. What are some of the expanding or growing occupations of the 1980s and 1990s?

8. *Using the information.*

Air pressure is caused by the weight of air from the outer limits or top of the atmosphere as it presses down upon the air below to the surface of the earth. Air pressure at sea level is about fifteen pounds per square inch. Human beings use air pressure as a force to lift water. For example, if air is kept from pressing against a certain part of the water, that part will be raised by the force of air pushing against the rest of the water. Can you think of times when we need to lift water by air pressure? We also use air that is compressed. This is forcing a large amount of air into a small, strong container. Then, we find that the air pressure is greatly increased and exerts pressure in all directions. Can you think of instances when we use air under pressure?

Shepherd

a. Why does the author ask two questions in the paragraph?
b. What principle about air and pressure is used with the automobile tire and by the gasoline motor?
c. What principle about air and pressure is illustrated by drinking a beverage with a straw?

The above suggestions and examples can be used as a guide as you select and prepare materials to improve reading comprehension.

Chapter 7
NEW WAYS OF THINKING
ABOUT READING INSTRUCTION*

Joseph Sanacore
Hauppauge School District
Hauppauge, Long Island, New York

Previous chapters concern important considerations for improving reading instruction. This chapter extends these considerations by focusing on three areas that can improve a student's reading performance. Prior knowledge, writing, and metacognition are aspects of process that reflect some of the demands made on readers as they interact with texts. Tutors should increase their awareness of these areas and should incorporate them into reading lessons at appropriate times.

Prior Knowledge and Reading

According to Pearson and Johnson (*1*), reading comprehension involves building bridges between what is new and what is known. This schema-theoretic view of comprehension is also noted by Adams and Bruce (*2*:23) who state, "Without prior knowledge, a complex object, such as a text, is not just difficult to interpret; strictly speaking, it is meaningless." The important relationship of prior knowledge (or schemata) and reading comprehension is further reinforced by Anderson, Pichert, and Shirey (*3*), Anderson, Spiro, and Anderson (*4*), Brown (*5*), Rumelhart (*6*), Rumelhart and Ortony (*7*), and Sanacore (*8, 9*).

*Parts of this chapter are adapted from Joseph Sanacore, "Improving Reading through Prior Knowledge and Writing," *Journal of Reading, 26,* May 1983, pp. 714-720; and Joseph Sanacore, "Metacognition and the Improvement of Reading: Some Important Links," *Journal of Reading,* in press. Reprinted with permission of Joseph Sanacore and the International Reading Association.

Additional support for prior knowledge and reading comprehension is provided by Stevens (*10*) who involved ninth grade students in the reading of paragraphs reflecting high knowledge and low knowledge topics. The researcher found that students with high prior knowledge of topics demonstrate excellent comprehension of material concerning those topics.

In another study, Stevens (*11*) provided tenth grade students with direct teaching of background knowledge. She wanted to determine if presenting students with a schema related to a topic would improve their understanding of material dealing with that topic. The results of her study support the idea "that teaching background knowledge of a topic to readers can improve their reading comprehension on material concerning that topic" (p. 328). Stevens' experiment also reinforces the theoretical view that background knowledge can be taught directly.

Unfortunately, few specific guidelines and strategies are available for helping students to become aware of their prior knowledge and to associate it with pertinent reading assignments. Of the worthwhile suggestions that do exist, Langer (*12*) presents a prereading plan referred to as PReP. This three step assessment/instructional procedure is designed for teacher use before the assigning of textbook reading. PReP is a small group discussion activity, involving about ten students. However, it also can be used on a one-to-one basis.

During the first phase, tutors guide learners to make initial associations with a key word, phrase, or picture selected from the text. For example, tutors might ask students to say anything that comes to mind when they hear the word *Congress*. As students respond, tutors write responses on the chalkboard.

During the second phase of PReP, learners are given opportunity to reflect on initial associations. Students reveal why they responded as they did in the first phase, and they increase awareness of their varied schemata. In addition, "they may weigh, reject, accept, revise, and integrate some of the ideas that come to mind" (p. 154).

During the third phase, students attempt to reformulate their knowledge of the material to be read. The tutor says, "Based on our discussion and before we read the text, have you any new ideas about...(e.g., *Congress*)?" (p. 154). Students' responses may reflect more elaboration, refinement, or revision, since they have had opportunity to think about their prior knowledge and place it within an appropriate structure.

The importance of PReP is that it is process-oriented. Especially noteworthy is the assessment aspect of this procedure which guides the tutor to 1) detemine the amount of information a reader has about a specific topic, as well as how the reader has organized this information; 2)become more aware of the language a student uses to express knowledge about a given subject; and 3) make judgments about how much additional background information and vocabulary are needed before students can successfully comprehend the text (p. 154). More discussion on prior knowledge and PReP can be found in Langer (13).

Similar to the intent of Langer's prereading plan is Thelen's model (14) for preparing students to read content reading assignments. Thelen combines the format of the structured overview and concept attainment. This combination helps tutors to guide students in organizing prior knowledge into conceptual frameworks, to fill informational gaps if they exist in students' backgrounds, and to blend these experiences with the new content students are about to read. Tutors can accomplish these outcomes by providing structured overviews, or graphic organizers, so that new concepts are clarified through the demonstration of conceptual relationships. The tutor, for example, motivates learners to assist with the development of a graphic hierarchy of a target concept. This hierarchy depicts the supraordinate, coordinate, and subordinate concepts. In addition, this structure provides examples and nonexamples as well as relevant and irrelevant attributes of the new target concept. Finally, as students demonstrate an understanding of the target concept, the tutor encourages them to generalize this understanding to new situations, such as additional concepts to be experienced in the reading assignment (15).

Another strategy for stimulating learners' prior knowledge is the PQ4R study procedure developed by Thomas and Robinson (16). This important procedure is based on the SQ3R approach (17), and it is supported by sound learning theory. *Preview, question, read, reflect, recite,* and *review* are the six steps that comprise PQ4R, and they "should be effective in improving the reading of chapter-length materials when the student's purpose is thorough understanding of the content. [They] should help the student comprehend better, concentrate better, and retain better" (pp. 136-137).

The preview step is supportive of the schema-theoretic view of comprehension, since it can activate readers' prior knowledge. The learner examines the title; reads the introductory statement thoroughly; glances over the subtitles, tables, charts, graphs, and captions; and reads the summary statement carefully. The preparatory experiences stimulate facility in comprehension, since they help learners to activate their previous knowledge of the content, to process selectively the textual information, and to predict aspects of the information that have not yet been experienced.

Other steps in PQ4R reinforce the *preview* step, since prior knowledge previously activated can be confirmed, bridged with new knowledge, and reconstructed. In addition, the overall PQ4R study procedure can help readers develop flexibility of schema shifting, especially as it relates to subthemes of textbook chapters.

Langer's description of PReP, Thelen's support of the structured overview, and Thomas and Robinson's discussion of PQ4R provide useful insights for helping readers integrate their prior knowledge with reading assignments. This integration was encouraged more than a decade ago by Ausubel (*18*) when he said, "The most important single factor influencing learning is what the learner already knows. Ascertain this and teach him accordingly" (p. vi). Ausubel's thought is stated rather strongly, but it certainly deserves consideration in the context of tutoring and learning.

Writing and Reading

The areas of writing and reading are viewed frequently as separate entities, unrelated to one other. This limited perception of communications usually results in fragmented curriculum development and isolated skill instruction. One way of preventing these negative outcomes is for the tutor to gain an understanding of aspects of written discourse. In attempting to create a psychological theory of discourse Brewer (*19*) surveys and gleans ideas from the academic disciplines of literary theory, rhetoric, and stylistics. Although he is concerned with a psychological perspective, his thoughtful insights have implications for understanding writing as a means of improving reading.

In his classification of written discourse, Brewer proposes three basic types: description, narration, and exposition. Each reflects an underlying cognitive structure and a surface structure. For example, descriptive discourse attempts to embody a stationary perceptual scene through a visual-spatial representation; this underlying cognitive representation is reflected to a degree with locatives, including *behind, above, near,* and *to the right of.* Narrative discourse attempts to demonstrate a series of events in time through a thematic or causal chain; this underlying structure tends to be comprised with terms, such as *while, then,* and *before.* Expository discourse attempts to represent abstract logical processes, presumably involving classification, comparison, and induction; this underlying logical structure seems to be organized with words, such as *because, since,* and *thus.*

In addition to the cognitive and surface structures reflecting each discourse type, Brewer's classification requires discourse forces. "The discourse force of a particular instance of discourse is an interaction of the communicative intent of the author and the perception of the reader" (p. 224). Brewer proposes four basic discourse forces: inform, entertain, persuade, and literary-aesthetic ("English does not seem to have an appropriate verb for this force," p. 224). In informative discourse, the author provides information. In entertaining discourse, the author attempts to excite, amuse, or frighten. In persuasive discourse, the author tries to convince the reader to adopt certain ideas or to do something. In literary-aesthetic discourse, the author attempts to provide the reader with an artistic experience and to have the reader view the discourse as an art form. Similar to the surface structure cues of the discourse types, surface cues also are represented to some extent in the discourse forces. Although these cues are not as clear for the discourse forces, some examples exist.

> Thus, if a scene is described as *a stand of coniferous saplings on a 50-meter moraine,* the discourse force is almost certain to be to inform. If the same scene is described as *a sublime sylvan knoll,* the discourse force is almost certain to be literary-aesthetic. If it is described as *a little old molehill dressed up fit to kill with pine trees,* the discourse force is almost certain to be to entertain (p. 226).

Brewer also provides some traditional genres in his psychological discourse classification. For the descriptive discourse: the informing force includes technical description, botany, and geography; the entertaining force involves ordinary description; the persuading force embodies house advertisement; and the literary-aesthetic force comprises poetic description. For the narrative discourse: the informing force involves newspaper story, history, instructions, recipes, and biography; the entertaining force includes mystery novel, western novel, science fiction novel, fairy tale, short story, biography, and light drama; the persuading force encompasses "message novel," parable, fable, advertisement, and drama; the literary-aesthetic force comprises literary novel, short story, and serious drama. For the expository discourse, only two forces are presented: the informing force includes scientific article, philosophy, and abstract definition; the persuading force involves sermon, propaganda, editorial, advertisement, and essay.

Since actual discourse is more varied and complex, Brewer admits that his classification scheme reflects a number of problems and a need for more elaborate theory development. Nonetheless, from an educational perspective, Brewer's ideas have valuable implications for the classroom. By encouraging students to identify and write various types of discourse (and discourse force), tutors can help these learners to understand different processes and constructs. This awareness can improve reading comprehension, since students gain insights and reinforce behaviors that are similar in both writing and reading.

These similarities are discussed poignantly by Petrosky (20) who focuses on the relationships among reading, response to literature, and composition. He argues that understanding is composing "and that the best representation of our understandings of texts begins with certain kinds of compositions" (p. 19). In this context, comprehension is viewed as an active process of reflecting explication, illustration, and critical analysis of perceptions and ideas. Thus, the putting together of meaning as individuals read is similar to the putting together of thoughts as they write. During reading, meaning is constructed both consciously and subconsciously; during writing, understanding of text is usually conscious.

Comprehension in both reading and composing, however, is dependent on learners' prior knowledge. Here, schemata take on Bartlett's definition (21) which includes not only cognitive factors but also affective aspects, such as personal awareness, feelings, and experiences. These considerations, as they relate to prior knowledge, support the reader response theory of interpreting text. Such a theory stresses the belief that comprehension takes place when reader and text interact. This belief differs from the traditional view of comprehension which considers meaning to be fixed in text and to be retrieved by the reader. (However, retrieving or locating information is certainly one part of comprehension.)

The reader response view of comprehension is exciting but also raises serious questions about shallow versus substantive understanding of text. To set appropriate standards for interpretation, Petrosky recommends Bleich's response heuristic (22). This process helps readers write about their comprehension of discourse, as they blend aspects of their personality and of the world as they perceive it. With this foundation established, students can become involved in critical discussions that lead to an analysis of their readings and of the process that informs them. Petrosky also gives examples of some of his students' responses to literature, and he describes shallow responses as well as substantive uses of the response heuristic. He considers poor responses to be sketchy, unfocused, narrow, and lacking in explanation and description as they relate to previous personal knowledge. Conversely, good responses include specific retellings of the text, explicit connections between personal associations and interpretations of the text, and generalizations from the discussion. Thus, good responses demonstrate good comprehension by revealing students' "mental maps" that guide their responses. Described another way, good responses reflect students' ability to "flesh out the personal knowledge and critical judgments that inform them" (p. 35). To accomplish these important outcomes, tutors are encouraged to read and write with their students, guiding them to realize that comprehension of text is like an act of composition.

In addition to Petrosky's noteworthy ideas, Robinson (*23*) presents excellent suggestions that have merit for integrating the reading and writing processes in the content areas. He focuses on major patterns and also presents pertinent examples of each pattern. Although he is primarily concerned with helping students improve their reading comprehension, his suggested patterns and examples serve as excellent clues to the kinds of writing students can pursue. As students increase their awareness of the similarities in reading and writing, they also increase their potential for understanding paragraph functions. These insights when integrated with learners' affective and cognitive backgrounds can lead to improved comprehension. The following outline shows Robinson's suggested writing patterns for some of the subject areas:

1. Science
   Enumeration
   Classification
   Generalization
   Problem solution
   Comparison or contrast
   Sequence
2. Social Studies
   Topic development
   Enumeration
   Generalization
   Sequence
   Comparison or contrast
   Effect-cause
   Question-answer
3. Mathematics
   Concept development
   Principle development
   Problem solution

In addition to these content areas, Robinson discusses writing patterns for English, business, driver education, health, home economics, and industrial arts (*24*).

Brewer's classification of written discourse types, Petrosky's focus on the relationships between writing and reading, and Robinson's presentation of writing patterns for the content areas have positive implications for tutoring and learning. For example, the tutor can visualize more clearly that writing and reading complement each other and therefore should not be treated as separate entities. This philosophy demonstrates to students that comprehending text is facilitated by a broader understanding of communications.

Metacognition and Reading

As individuals become increasingly aware of processes involved in the comprehension act, they can exercise degrees of control over some of these processes. Such conscious control is referred to as metacognition, and this area has the potential for improving reading performance.

According to *A Dictionary of Reading and Related Terms* (*25*), *metacognition* is defined as "those theories and principles used in the study of thought processes" (p. 196). Flavell (*26*:p. 232) elaborated on metacognition by indicating that it

> refers to one's knowledge concerning one's own cognitive processes and products or anything related to them, e.g., the learning-relevant properties of information or data. For example, I am engaging in metacognition (metamemory, metalearning, metaattention, metalanguage, or whatever) if I notice that I am having more trouble learning *A* than *B*; if it strikes me that I should double-check *C* before accepting it as a fact; if it occurs to me that I had better scrutinize each and every alternative in any multiple-choice type task situation before deciding which is the best one; if I sense that I had better make a note of *D* because I may forget it. . . . Metacognition refers, among other things, to the active monitoring and consequent regulation and orchestration of these processes in relation to the cognitive objects or data on which they bear, usually in the service of some concrete goal or objective.

These definitions when applied to the reading act provide useful insights about the dynamics of understanding text. Although extensive research on metacognition and reading has not yet been conducted, Brown (*27*) presented empirical examples of efficient learners' growing awareness and control of their intended study skills and capacities. In this context, Brown linked aspects of metacognition and reading. For example, in "Knowing When You Know," the reader monitors the degree of understanding or the lack of understanding; this basic form of self-awareness is essential since recognizing failure to comprehend is prerequisite to employing strategies to eliminate the comprehension block. In "Knowing What You Know," learners are aware of the knowledge they already possess and are able to operate on this knowledge; implicit in these characteristics is facility in predicting what is known (even when immediate recall has failed) and what is not known. In "Knowing What You Need to Know," readers are conscious of certain types of information needed to complete a task effectively; this outcome is achieved with more ease and efficiency when students know the purposes of the task. In "Knowing the Utility of Active Intervention," readers know that active strategies, such as categorization and rehearsal, are useful in achieving better performance; however, preliminary data suggest that although students may be aware of the importance of active strategies, they may not adopt them during the actual reading and studying of prose. Brown also discussed the importance of "Study - Time Utilization" and focused on learners' problems in selecting and studying main ideas, choosing suitable retrieval cues, and estimating readiness for tests.

An important aspect of active comprehension (and of metacognition) is the ability to generate good questions during the studying of prose material. Andre and Anderson (28) attempted to demonstrate that 1) students can be taught to locate important main points in text and to develop questions related to them and 2) self-generation of such questions will facilitate understanding the text. The researchers found that high school students who were trained to generate main idea questions developed more good questions and produced greater learning than students who were not trained in this skill. One explanation concerning the effectiveness of the main idea self-questioning method is reflected in the combination of metacognitive and cognitive characteristics. For example, the "self-generation of questions may be an effective reading strategy because the student is forced to a) pause frequently, b) deal with an 'understanding question,' c) determine whether comprehension has occurred, and d) decide what strategic action should be taken. The process of self-awareness and conscious control of the study activity is an illustration of the metacognitive aspect involved in the self-questioning strategy" (p. 620). Interestingly, Andre and Anderson found that low and middle ability students seemed to benefit more from the self-questioning training than high verbal ability students. According to the investigators, learners with verbal facility already knew how to develop good comprehension questions, while those who did not possess such facility demonstrated less adequate study behaviors. Thus, low and middle verbal ability students improved their performance probably because they engaged in a study technique that was more effective than the study method they usually use.

Another study concerning metacognitive aspects of self-questioning was conducted by Singer and Donlan (29). Eleventh grade students were randomly assigned to an experimental group and taught a problem-solving schema for understanding complex short stories; this schema included the stories' plan, goal, action, obstacles, and outcomes representing success or failure. Students were guided to learn this schema with related schema-general questions, to use the schema-general questions to create their own story-specific questions, and to read with the purpose of answering their own questions. The control group read to answer story-specific questions posed by the teacher. The results of the study supported the experimental treatment, since students learned to apply to complex narrative text a problem solving schema and its related components; in addition, the students significantly improved their comprehension of complex short stories. The investigators cautioned, however, that the difference between the experimental and control groups was not evident until the third instructional session. This caution has implications for both research and practice because it reinforces the belief that effective instruction must continue for more than one session, "so that students can learn these complex metacognitive processes and have practice in applying them" (p. 179).

Related to metacognition and reading are the monitoring and resolving of comprehension obstacles. Garner and Reis (30) investigated the effects of spontaneous text lookbacks on eliminating comprehension blocks. Students in grades four through ten (M = grade seven) served as poor-comprehender subjects. Learners in grades six through eight (M = grade seven) were chosen as good comprehenders; this second group was similar to the first group in most areas except reading proficiency. Students read a narrative passage consisting of three paragraphs with questions following each paragraph. Some of the questions required students to look back and retrieve information from an earlier part of the passage. During the experiment, students' verbal and nonverbal behaviors were observed. The researchers analyzed the results and found that poor comprehenders mostly did not show monitoring and did not spontaneously use lookbacks. Good comprehenders in grade eight showed monitoring and used lookbacks. Thus, good comprehenders recognized a block to comprehension; only the oldest good comprehenders were able to determine if something could be done about the failure to comprehend and were able to engage in resolving activities. The findings of this study also suggested that only eighth grade good comprehenders are likely to use lookback strategies regularly during independent reading settings.

Since metacognition is also concerned with the development of study skills, Adams, Carnine, and Gersten (31) explored the use of a study strategy based on the SQ3R method, aspects of task analysis, and direct instruction. Fifth grade students who had adequate decoding skills but ineffective study skills comprised the target population. Three instructional groups, consisting of fifteen students in each, were exposed to different training procedures. The *systematic instruction* group learned to apply a study method variation which included previewing the headings and subheadings of a passage, reciting the subheadings, asking questions from the subheadings about what might be important to learn, reading to locate answers to the questions and to locate other important details, and rereading the subheadings and reciting important related information. When the entire passage was read, the *systematic instruction* group reviewed by reading each subheading and recalling important related information. The independent study with feedback group focused on traditional seatwork; for example, the students studied a passage independently until they thought they learned the important information. The *no instruction* group remained in regular classrooms and did not receive exposure to either of the above training procedures. An analysis of the results indicated that on immediate and delayed short answer tests, the *systematic instruction* group performed at a significantly higher level than the other two groups; no significant difference was observed between the *independent study with feedback* group and the *no instruction* group. In addition, observations of students' study behaviors in the *systematic instruction* group support the efficacy of teaching the metacognitive skills of attending to subheadings, of pausing to reread, of reviewing after reading, and of taking notes.

Another pertinent study was conducted by Meyer, Brandt, and Bluth (32). These researchers focused on ninth grade students' use of the structure strategy which emphasized following the top level organization of text to remember important information. A representative sample of students had been divided into good, average, and poor comprehender groups, based on these students' standardized achievement test performance and based on teachers' ratings. Expository passages reflecting comparison and problem/solution top level structures were selected for the study. Meyer's prose analysis procedure (*33, 34*) was used to identify the passages' top level structures. In addition, with-signaling and without signaling versions of the passages were written. The with-signaling version explicitly stated the top level structure and provided underlined words that signaled pertinent information to the reader. The without-signaling version did not include these aspects. Students were assigned to the different versions of the passages through a stratified random assignment procedure. They read versions of the passages and then recorded as much related information as they could recall. The following week, students again recorded all the information they remembered about the passages. They also completed a recognition test concerning the passages. The findings of the study demonstrated that only 22 percent of the students sampled used the structure strategy consistently, and less than 50 percent used the strategy at least once. However, most students considered good comprehenders employed the top level structure effectively, while most individuals considered poor comprehenders did not. Another finding indicated that those who used the strategy recalled more information than those who did not. In addition, use of the strategy led to better discrimination between information consistent with passage semantics and intruded information.

Since aspects of metacognition can improve reading performance, tutors should pursue strategies that link these two areas. The following suggestions are not exhaustive but provide some direction blending metacognition and reading:

1. Teach students (especially those with low and middle verbal abilities) to generate questions during the reading and studying of expository text. Students can be taught to recognize the main ideas of paragraphs, to develop questions relating to the main ideas but reflecting new examples of the concepts presented in the instructional materials, and to paraphrase the questions about the concepts if the new examples are inappropriate. These criteria represent "good student-generated comprehension questions," and similar criteria were used in the Andre and Anderson study. Students would benefit from initial exposure to model paragraphs with accompanying questions generated by the tutor. Then, learners should experience single paragraphs and also longer passages and should have opportunities to construct "good" questions related to these materials.

2. Teach students to create story-specific questions from schema-general questions during the reading of complex narrative text. For example, Donlan and Singer (35) presented schema-general questions concerning a short story's leading character (Who is the leading character?), the goal (What does this leading character appear to be striving for?), the obstacles (What is the first obstacle the character encounters?), the outcome (Does the character reach the original goal or the revised goal or no goal?), and the theme (This story basically shows a person's struggle with. . .). These and other schema-general questions are useful for helping students comprehend better the structure and content of short stories. As narrative text becomes more complex, however, students can benefit from learning to convert story-general questions to story-specific questions and from reading to answer their questions. The illustration, adapted from the Singer and Donlan study, shows schema-general questions from which students generated story-specific questions.

Schema-General Questions	Story-Specific Questions
Who is the leading character?	Is this story going to be more about the officer or the barber?
What is the leading character trying to accomplish in the story?	Will the barber kill the officer with the razor?
What stands in the way of the leading character reaching the desired goal?	Will the officer be a willing victim? (p. 173)

3. Teach students to monitor and resolve blocks to comprehension. Using a passage that a reader can decode proficiently, the tutor intersperses questions in text. Some of the questions would require students to look back at previously read paragraphs to retrieve information. These lookback questions should be constructed so that answers sought are not automatically resolvable, or else no lookback behavior would be necessary. On the other hand, care should be taken in developing the questions and in interspersing them in text so that the flow of meaning is not disrupted significantly. To observe lookback behavior more easily, the tutor presents the passage on separate sheets with a paragraph on the top and questions on the bottom of each sheet. Some of the questions should require readers to look back, while other questions may be answered with relative ease. After reading each paragraph, students are asked questions. Completed paragraphs are placed at a ninety degree angle to students so that they are encouraged to reread this material and the observer is able to monitor lookback behavior. In addition, the

observer constantly views both verbal and nonverbal behaviors. According to Patterson, Cosgrove, and O'Brien (*36*), nonverbal measures can reflect comprehension or lack of comprehension. Thus, lookbacks, actual corrections, eye contact with direction-giver, grunts, long response hesitations, and facial distortions should be noted. Although these suggestions are adapted from the Garner and Reis study, they are useful as individualized instructional techniques. Students should be encouraged to use lookback and resolving strategies regularly when comprehension blocks occur during instructional and independent reading settings. Students should be motivated to "1) recognize that a failure has occurred, 2) decide whether to do something about the failure at that time, and 3) engage (conditional upon step two) in fixup activities which supply the prerequisite information" (*37*, p. 199).

4. Teach students about the structure of textbook chapters and guide them to use strategies that increase their abilities in comprehending text and retrieving information. These strategies should direct students' attention to the organizational aspects of the material and should guide students to avoid reading the material nonstop. Using textbooks with consistently organized chapters, students can learn to apply SQ3R, PQ4R, PQRST, or another variation similar to the one used in the Adams, Carnine, and Gersten study. Study procedures such as these can improve students' understanding and retention of information when the procedures are applied to reading materials reflecting subheadings or clear topic statements; when students generate questions from the subheadings; when students read and recite important information related to the subheadings; and when students rehearse the entire chapter, section by section, until they decide further study is unnecessary. These outcomes suggest that readers know their own intellectual processes, since they demonstrate conscious awareness of what is important to study, how to study, and how much studying is needed (*38*). Thus, learners are provided with a means of monitoring the efficiency of their reading and studying.

5. Teach students to learn and recall valuable information by adhering to the text structure. Using well-organized passages with recognizable top level structures and suitable reading levels, students can benefit from a systematic guide that helps them determine what is important to remember. However, in the Meyer, Brandt, and Bluth study, the researchers indicated that adhering to an author's text structure may be a developmental process requiring exposure to different discourse

types in the following sequence: "Stories, description, antecendent/ consequent, problem/solution, and comparison (argumentative text)" (p. 98). Initial sensitivity to these top level structures may be learned with greater ease if the passages are presented to students with underlined words of signaling. Thus, in a problem/solution passage consisting of two paragraphs, the first paragraph might show underlined words, such as *problem, for example,* and *also;* the second paragraph might contain underlined words, including *solution, first, second,* and *third* (pp. 102-103). As students develop facility identifying top level structures, they should be exposed to passages with no underlined words of signaling.

Appropriate use of metacognitive strategies during reading suggests that reading comprehension reflects active processes and that students are exercising degrees of control over these processes. In addition, the potential is increased for upgrading reading performance.

Summary

The scope of this chapter is limited to improving reading through prior knowledge, writing, and metacognition. These aspects of process support the idea that success in reading as well as in communications is more likely to occur when synthesis rather than fragmentation is encouraged. Although instructional implications are stressed, evaluative considerations are implied; therefore, the checklist titled "Some Schema-Theoretic, Writing, and Metacognitive Guidelines for Improving Reading Lessons" (*39*) may remind tutors, teachers, and administrators of important suggestions that should be planned cooperatively for reading lessons.

Some Schema-Theoretic, Writing, and Metacognitive Guidelines for Improving Reading Lessons

	Indicate frequency of occurrence of each guideline			
Never	Rarely	Sometimes	Usually	Always

PReP

1. Tutor plans to use PReP by selecting a word, phrase, or picture concerning a major concept in the text	1	2	3	4	5
2. Tutor uses PReP and records valuable information concerning learners' responses to:					
• What comes to your mind when you hear or see the word, phrase, or picture...?	1	2	3	4	5
• What made you think of that...?	1	2	3	4	5
• Have you any new ideas about...?	1	2	3	4	5
3. Tutor assesses students' levels of response and determines if students possess much, some, or little knowledge about a given concept	1	2	3	4	5
4. Tutor considers students' levels of knowledge for instructional purposes by:					
• Assigning appropriate reading materials to learners who possess much or some knowledge	1	2	3	4	5
• Giving guidance to students who have some knowledge by asking them probing questions	1	2	3	4	5
• Providing direct instruction of a relevant concept to individuals who possess little knowledge of the concept	1	2	3	4	5

Structured Overview

5. Tutor guides students to assist with the development of a graphic hierarchy of a target concept that depicts:					
• Supraordinate concepts	1	2	3	4	5
• Coordinate concepts	1	2	3	4	5
• Subordinate concepts	1	2	3	4	5

	Indicate frequency of occurrence of each guideline				
	Never	Rarely	Sometimes	Usually	Always

6. Tutor provides learners with:

	N	R	S	U	A
• Examples of the target concept	1	2	3	4	5
• Nonexamples of the target concept	1	2	3	4	5
• Relevant attributes of the target concept	1	2	3	4	5
• Irrelevant attributes of the target concept	1	2	3	4	5

7. Tutor encourages students to generalize their understanding of the target concept to new situations.

1	2	3	4	5

PQ4R

8. Tutor motivates learners to activate their prior knowledge by applying the *preview* step in PQ4R to content area reading assignments, so that:

• The title is examined	1	2	3	4	5
• The introductory statement is read thoroughly	1	2	3	4	5
• The subtitles, graphs, charts, tables, and captions are glanced over	1	2	3	4	5
• The summary statement is read carefully	1	2	3	4	5

9. Tutor guides learners to apply other steps in PQ4R (*question, read, reflect, recite,* and *review*) to content area reading assignments, so that knowledge previously activated during the *preview* step is confirmed, is bridged with new knowledge, is reconstructed.

1	2	3	4	5

10. Tutor encourages students to use PQ4R to develop flexibility of schema shifting of subthemes in textbook chapters.

1	2	3	4	5

N e v e r	R a r e l y	S o m e t i m e s	U s u a l l y	A l w a y s

Discourse Types

11. Tutor presents models and examples of the
following discourse types and discourse
forces, so that students learn to identify and
write them and thus improve their reading
comprehension:

	N	R	S	U	A
• Descriptive discourse with an informing force (e.g., technical, descriptive, botany, and geography)	1	2	3	4	5
• Descriptive discourse with an entertaining force (e.g., ordinary description)	1	2	3	4	5
• Descriptive discourse with a persuading force (e.g., house advertisement)	1	2	3	4	5
• Descriptive discourse with a literary-aesthetic force (e.g., poetic description)	1	2	3	4	5
• Narrative discourse with an informing force (e.g., newspaper story, history, instructions, recipes, and biography)	1	2	3	4	5
• Narrative discourse with an entertaining force (e.g., mystery novel, western novel, science fiction novel, fairy tale, short story, biography, and "light" drama)	1	2	3	4	5
• Narrative discourse with a persuading force (e.g., "message novel," parable, fable, advertisement, and drama)	1	2	3	4	5
• Narrative discourse with a literary-aesthetic force(e.g., literary novel, short story, and "serious" drama)	1	2	3	4	5
• Expository discourse with an informing force (e.g., scientific article, philosophy, and abstract definition)	1	2	3	4	5
• Expository discourse with a persuading force (e.g., sermon, propaganda, editorial, advertisement, and essay)	1	2	3	4	5

	Indicate frequency of occurrence of each guideline				
	Never	Rarely	Sometimes	Usually	Always

Response Heuristic

12. Tutor guides learners to realize similarities of reading and writing by encouraging learners to write about their understanding of text while including:

	Never	Rarely	Sometimes	Usually	Always
• Specific retellings of the text	1	2	3	4	5
• Explicit connections between personal associations and interpretations of the text	1	2	3	4	5
• Generalizations from the discussion	1	2	3	4	5

Writing Patterns

13. Tutor motivates students to integrate reading and writing processes by:

	Never	Rarely	Sometimes	Usually	Always
• Presenting examples of major writing patterns for the content areas	1	2	3	4	5
• Stimulating learners to read the writing patterns and to develop a feel for the way they are constructed	1	2	3	4	5
• Assisting individuals to construct passages similar to the writing patterns	1	2	3	4	5

Question Generation

14. Tutor helps learners to create questions for expository paragraphs and passages by:

	Never	Rarely	Sometimes	Usually	Always
• Recognizing the main ideas	1	2	3	4	5
• Developing questions relating to the main ideas but reflecting new examples of the concepts presented in the instructional materials	1	2	3	4	5
• Paraphrasing the questions about the concepts if the new examples are inappropriate	1	2	3	4	5

	N e v e r	R a r e l y	S o m e t i m e s	U s u a l l y	A l w a y s

Indicate frequency of occurrence of each guideline

15. Tutor guides students to develop story-specific questions from schema-general questions during the reading of a complex short story's:

	N	R	S	U	A
• Leading character	1	2	3	4	5
• Goal	1	2	3	4	5
• Obstacles	1	2	3	4	5
• Outcome	1	2	3	4	5
• Theme	1	2	3	4	5

Monitoring and Resolving Comprehension Blocks

16. Tutor teaches individuals to monitor and resolve blocks to comprehension by:

	N	R	S	U	A
• Using a passage the reader can decode proficiently	1	2	3	4	5
• Interspersing questions in the text so that some of the answers are not automatically resolvable	1	2	3	4	5
• Observing verbal and nonverbal behaviors of students as they answer the questions	1	2	3	4	5

17. Tutor motivates individuals to:

	N	R	S	U	A
• Recognize that a comprehension block has occurred	1	2	3	4	5
• Decide whether to take action at that time	1	2	3	4	5
• Engage in appropriate activities (if needed) which supply the necessary data	1	2	3	4	5

	Never	Rarely	Sometimes	Usually	Always

Text Structure

18. Tutor increases students' awareness of the structure of textbook chapters by:

	Never	Rarely	Sometimes	Usually	Always
• Directing students' attention to the organizational aspects of chapters	1	2	3	4	5
• Reminding students to avoid reading the chapters nonstop	1	2	3	4	5
• Guiding students to use strategies such as SQ3R, PQ4R, and PQRST	1	2	3	4	5

19. Tutor helps learners to adhere to the author's text structure by:

	Never	Rarely	Sometimes	Usually	Always
• Using well-organized passages with recognizable top level structures and suitable reading levels	1	2	3	4	5
• Presenting the passages initially with underlined words of signaling	1	2	3	4	5
• Using passages with no underlined words of signaling when students demonstrate facility identifying top level structures	1	2	3	4	5

References
1. Pearson, P. David, & Dale Johnson. *Teaching Reading Comprehension.* New York: Macmillan, 1978.
2. Adams, Marilyn J., & Bertram Bruce. "Background Knowledge and Reading Comprehension." In Judith A. Langer & M. Trika Smith-Burke (Eds.), *Reader Meets Author/Bridging the Gap: A Psycholinguistic and Sociolinguistic Perspective.* Newark, Delaware: International Reading Association, 1982, 2-25.
3. Anderson, Richard C., James W. Pichert, & Larry L. Shirey. *Effects of the Reader's Schema at Different Points in Time.* Arlington, Virginia: Eric Document Reproduction Service, 1979. (ED 169 523)
4. Anderson, Richard C., Rand Spiro, & Michael Anderson. "Schemata as Scaffolding for the Representation of Information in Connected Discourse." *American Educational Research Journal, 15* (Winter 1978), 433-440.

5. Brown, Ann. *Knowing When, Where, and How to Remember: A Problem of Meta-cognition.* Technical Report No. 47. Urbana, Illinois: Center for the Study of Reading, University of Illinois, 1977.
6. Rumelhart, David. "Schemata: The Building Blocks of Cognition." In Rand Spiro, Bertram Bruce, & William Brewer (Eds.), *Theoretical Issues in Reading Comprehension: Perspectives from Cognitive Psychology, Linguistics, Artificial Intelligence, and Education.* Hillsdale, New Jersey: Erlbaum, 1980, 33-58.
7. Rumelhart, David, & Andrew Ortony. "The Representation of Knowledge in Memory." In Richard C. Anderson, Rand Spiro, & William E. Montague (Eds.), *Schooling and the Acquisition of Knowledge.* Hillsdale, New Jersey: Erlbaum, 1977. 99-135.
8. Sanacore, Joseph. "Evaluating the Teaching of Reading in the Content Areas." Paper presented at the Twenty-Eighth Annual Convention of the International Reading Association, Anaheim, California, 1983.
9. Sanacore, Joseph. "Transferring the PQ4R Study Procedure: Administrative Concerns," *The Clearing House, 55* (January 1982), 234-236.
10. Stevens, Kathleen C. "The Effect of Background Knowledge on the Reading Comprehension of Ninth Graders," *Journal of Reading Behavior, 12* (1980), 151-154.
11. Stevens, Kathleen C. "Can We Improve Reading by Teaching Background Knowledge?" *Journal of Reading, 25* (January 1982), 326-329.
12. Langer, Judith A. "From Theory to Practice: A Prereading Plan," *Journal of Reading, 25* (November 1981), 152-156.
13. Langer, Judith A. "Facilitating Text Processing: The Elaboration of Prior Knowledge." In Judith A. Langer & M. Trika Smith-Burke (Eds.), *Reader Meets Author/Bridging the Gap: A Psycholinguistic and Sociolinguistic Perspective.* Newark, Delaware: International Reading Association, 1982, 149-162.
14. Thelen, Judith. "Preparing Students for Content Reading Assignments." *Journal of Reading, 25* (March 1982), 544-549.
15. Frayer, Dorothy, W.G. Frederick, & Herbert Klausmeier. *A Schema for Testing the Level of Cognitive Mastery.* Working Paper No. 16. Madison, Wisconsin: Wisconsin Research and Development Center for Cognitive Learning, 1969.
16. Thomas, Ellen Lamar, & H. Alan Robinson. *Improving Reading in Every Class: A Sourcebook for Teachers* (2nd ed.). Boston: Allyn and Bacon, 1977.
17. Robinson, Francis P. *Effective Reading.* New York: Harper and Row, 1962.
18. Ausubel, David. *Educational Psychology: A Cognitive View.* New York: Holt, Rinehart and Winston, 1968.
19. Brewer, William. "Literacy Theory, Rhetoric, and Stylistics: Implications for Psychology." In Rand, Spiro, Bertram Bruce, & William Brewer (Eds.), *Theoretical Issues in Reading Comprehension: Perspectives from Cognitive Psychology, Linguistics, Artificial Intelligence, and Education.* Hillsdale, New Jersey: Erlbaum, 1980, 221-239.
20. Petrosky, Anthony R. "From Story to Essay: Reading and Writing," *College Composition and Communication, 33* (February 1982), 19-36.
21. Bartlett, F.C. *Remembering.* London: Cambridge University Press, 1932.
22. Bleich, David. *Subjective Criticism.* Baltimore: Johns Hopkins University Press, 1978.
23. Robinson, H. Alan. *Teaching Reading, Writing, and Study Strategies: The Content Areas.* Boston: Allyn and Bacon, 1983.
24. Sanacore, Joseph. "Schoolwide Writing Strategies," *The Clearing House, 53* (April 1980), 391-393.
25. Harris, Theodore L., & Richard E. Hodges (Eds.). *A Dictionary of Reading and Related Terms.* Newark, Delaware: International Reading Association, 1981.
26. Flavell, J.H. "Metacognitive Aspects of Problem Solving," in L.B. Resnick (Ed.), *The Nature of Intelligence.* Hillsdale, New Jersey: Erlbaum, 1976, 196.

27. Brown, Ann L. "Metacognitive Development and Reading," in Rand J. Spiro, Bertram Bruce, & William F. Brewer (Eds.), *Theoretical Issues in Reading Comprehension,* pp. 453-481. Hillsdale, New Jersey: Erlbaum, 1980.

28. Andre, Marli E.D.A., & Thomas H. Anderson. "The Development and Evaluation for a Self-Questioning Study Technique," *Reading Research Quarterly, 14* (1978-1979), 605-623.

29. Singer, Harry, & Dan Donlan. "Active Comprehension: Problem-Solving Schema with Question Generation for Comprehension of Complex Short Stories," *Reading Research Quarterly, 17* (1982), 166-186.

30. Garner, Ruth, & Ron Reis. "Monitoring and Resolving Comprehension Obstacles: An Investigation of Spontaneous Text Lookbacks among Upper Grade Good and Poor Comprehenders," *Reading Research Quarterly, 16* (1981), 569-582.

31. Adams, Abby, Douglas Carnine, & Russell Gersten. "Instructional Strategies for Studying Content Area Texts in the Intermediate Grades," *Reading Research Quarterly, 18* (1982), 27-55.

32. Meyer, Bonnie J.F., David M. Brandt, & George J. Bluth. "Use of Top Level Structure in Text: Key for Reading Comprehension of Ninth Grade Students," *Reading Research Quarterly, 16* (1980), 72-103.

33. Meyer, Bonnie J.F. "Identification of the Structure of Prose and Its Implications for the Study of Reading Memory," *Journal of Reading Behavior, 7* (1975), 7-47.

34. Meyer, Bonnie J.F. *The Organization of Prose and Its Effects on Memory.* Amsterdam: North-Holland Publishing, 1975.

35. Donlan, Dan, & Harry Singer. "Active Comprehension of Short Stories." In M.P. Douglass (Ed.), *Forty-Third Yearbook of the Claremont Reading Conference.* Claremont, California: Claremont Reading Conference, 1979.

36. Patterson, C.J., J.M. Cosgrove, & R.G. O'Brien. "Nonverbal Indicants of Comprehension and Noncomprehension in Children," *Developmental Psychology, 16* (1980), 38-48.

37. Alessi, S.M., T.H. Anderson, & E.T. Goetz. "An Investigation of Lookbacks During Studying," *Discourse Processes, 2* (1979), 197-212.

38. Flavell, J.H., & H.M. Wellman. "Metamemory," in R.V. Kail & J.W. Hagen (Eds.), *Perspectives on the Development of Memory and Cognition.* Hillsdale, New Jersey: Erlbaum, 1977.

39. Sanacore, Joseph. "Improving Reading in Secondary Curricular Areas: Plans for Implementing and Supervising Instruction in Content Classes," invited presentation at the Administrators Conference of the Nassau Reading Council and the Nassau Association of District Curriculum Officials, Hofstra University, 1982.

Chapter 8
ORGANIZING THE VOLUNTEER TUTOR PROGRAM

Lenore Sandel
Hofstra University

Now that one has some understanding of the principles, practices, and materials needed in a volunteer program, the next question is "How does one organize and administer such a program?" This chapter presents procedures and forms desirable for the step-by-step administration of the program. These are suggested forms and procedures. Your own practical situation will determine the revisions. A description of a structured volunteer program is included; the specific information provides useful suggestions which may be adapted for any particular, local community program.

The Volunteer Tutor Application
(see Form A)

The sample application provides for a brief statement in writing about the volunteer's preparation for tutoring. Both professional and volunteer experiences are to be considered in the assignment of tutor to student.

If the tutor-student assignments are to be realistic and mutually rewarding, the information submitted by both must be considered by the coordinator or administrator of the program.

The Student Application and Interview
(see Forms B and C)

It is suggested that the interviewer be an individual other than the tutor in order to provide objective evaluation and placement and that the interviewer be qualified in administering the intake interview and any other diagnostic instrument to be used. Professionals who train the tutors, participating school personnel, or selected volunteers who have been prepared for this initial and important step may serve as interviewers.

The initial interview in this program is an integral, and frequently the only, instrument of diagnosis. If the student's lack of skill precludes any use of printed materials, informal or standardized, the information gained during the interview must lead to an estimate of general intelligence, experiential background, verbal ability, and emotional and social response to the total situation.

Two examples of applications follow:

Application 1 (Form B). This brief form can be used for students who are able to provide a minimum of written information. Interviewers should offer to assist students by clarifying questions if necessary. If students appear to be having difficulty or give evidence of frustration, interviewers should "talk" about the questions and enter the suggestions for them. After Application 1 is completed, interviewers can continue with the longer form (Application 2) and complete the remaining information.

Application 2 (Form C). When a client is unable to fill in the information on Application 1, Application 2 should be used as the basis of the interview.

The following guidelines can aid in increasing the diagnostic value of the interview: 1) the location and nature of formal education are significant since school districts and geographic areas differ in standards and curriculum; 2) the students' reason for entering the program should be a principal factor in the selection and preparation of instructional materials: i.e., students who seek to pass a driver's test to qualify for a position should be given relevant materials as a basis of instruction; 3) the physical condition of students (vision, hearing, motor coordination) should be noted for both casual and remedial implications; 4) environmental factors, such as marital status, family members living at home, and number of children, suggest the amount of supplemental work which may be expected; and 5— age and occupation of students may determine the goals and duration and nature of instruction.

It is particularly important to keep in mind that students have found sufficient initiative and reason to seek help in reading. The essence of this motivation must be encouraged, sustained, and reinforced with confidence borne of successful experiences.

Sandel

Assignment Sheet (Form D)

The interviewer-diagnostician, in entering such information as reading level and chief areas of difficulty, should include all relevant observations made during the intake interview. The coordinator of the program, in assigning student to tutor, must necessarily consider all entries of the interviewer as they relate to the particular skills of the tutor; i.e., a student with limited verbal ability or withdrawn behavior should be assigned to a tutor adept at eliciting responses.

A copy of the assignment sheet, together with all subsequent information, should be kept on file in the client's folder.

Lesson Plan (Form E)

The sample lesson plan outline given here is designed to include those aspects of any lesson which are fundamental in recommended teaching procedures. The plan is to be prepared prior to each teaching assignment and should provide activities commensurate with the time allotment of the session. Tutor preparation gives structure to the scope of the student's instruction and provides maximum use of time, energy, and materials through purposeful planning.

Tutors, however prepared as they may be with a specific plan, must be flexible in approaches and sufficiently familiar with their students' needs to adjust a particular lesson to meet other spontaneous motivation. Since one is primarily concerned here with adult or mature students, practical, everyday situations in their lives are frequently introduced in a teaching assignment. The tutor's ability to utilize this motivation is an important aspect of successful teaching since it can reinforce instruction as well as stimulate new learning. For example, a tutor may be prepared with a lesson plan for teaching word structure as an aid to word meaning. The material may be related to vocational interest in auto mechanics; the student, concerned with his/her application for medical insurance, appears for the lesson. The tutor, in assisting the student with reading the new material, can use selected portions of the prepared lesson plan in reviewing skills and in teaching the new skill.

Sections of the Lesson Plan (Form E)

Review. It is recommended in a developmental lesson and emphasized in a remedial situation that a review of the previous lesson precede the teaching of a new skill. The review at the onset of the lesson, therefore, maintains both continuity in the total program through reinforcement and reteaching when necessary.

Readiness. This preparation for the specific lesson relates to a discussion of the subject material to be used and the identification and relationship of the student's background of experience to the subject under discussion.

Specific purpose. Specific purpose refers to the single lesson to be taught. The purpose may relate to a particular phonic element (consonant blend or vowel sound), structural analysis (prefixes, suffixes, syllabication), or comprehension skill (finding the main idea of a paragraph). This specific purpose aids tutors in selecting, noting, and guiding themselves in limiting each lesson while structuring the sequence of lessons.

General purpose. The general purpose of long range goals gives scope and dimension to the teaching program and relates most directly to the initial diagnosis of student needs. The "screening" or intake interview and testing would suggest overall deficiencies, i.e., lack of decoding skills in using materials at a particular level, comprehension skills, or basic study techniques.

In those cases where the student is unable to be tested because of severe reading retardation, it can be assumed that instruction will proceed with basic decoding skills based on the client's listening and speaking vocabulary and experiential background.

Materials. It is likely that in working with adolescents or adults the materials used in instruction may vary from formal to informal (newspapers, magazines, tutor-made materials, vocational bulletins) to meet individual needs, purposes, and interests. The type of materials must be noted for two principal reasons: 1) to identify the selection for the tutor and student in the review, association, and application of reading skills and 2) to guide the program advisor in supervising and evaluating the instructional program.

Procedures. The tutor notes here the sequence of the lesson and/or any special approach to be used.

Evaluation. This evaluation provides information for the lesson to follow. The tutor notes the program which has been made before beginning the next lesson. Any approach or material that has been especially effective is mentioned here.

Contact Sheet (Form F)

Following each lesson, the tutor may record its purpose, materials, procedures, and evaluation. This information may be the same or similar to the lesson plan. It is this contact report which is important for the advisor's information as well as the tutor's projected teaching plans.

Suggested Forms

FORM A

Volunteer Tutor Application

NAME _____

ADDRESS _____

_____

TELEPHONE _____

Education:

*Institution (School   Course of Study   Date   Degree (or
or Organization)   or Major   Certificate of Competency)*

Professional Work:

Volunteer services:

Service   Sponsor   Date   Duration

What do you like to do in your free time?

Availability for tutoring program:

Days   Time   Transportation Car _____

Bus _____

Other _____

Please state any preference for student assignment: (Male, female, and age or grade level)

FORM B

Student Application #1

PLEASE FILL IN THE FOLLOWING:

YOUR NAME _____

YOUR HOME ADDRESS _____

_____

YOUR TELEPHONE NUMBER _____

Date of Birth _____ Place of Birth _____

Length of Schooling _____

Do you Work?   Yes _____ No _____

What kind of work do you do? _____

_____

What do you like to do in your spare time? _____

_____

Are you married?   Yes _____ No _____

Do you have any children?   Yes _____ No _____

How old are they? _____

Do your children live with you?   Yes _____ No _____

Why do you want reading help? _____

_____

When do you have free time?

Days_____ Hours _____

Sandel

FORM C

Student Application #2

Date of Application _____

Sex _____

NAME OF APPLICANT _____

ADDRESS OF APPLICANT _____

HOME TELEPHONE NUMBER _____

Date of Birth _____

Place of Birth _____

Occupation _____

Health _____

Vision _____

Hearing _____

Marital Status _____

Children of Applicant (sex and age) _____

Has applicant suffered from any serious illness or accident?

Yes _____ No _____

Illness _____ Date _____ Result _____

Has applicant attended school(s) for formal education? _____

School(s) _____ Location _____

Grade and/or Date _____

Does the applicant read or examine any magazines and/or newspapers

regularly? _____ Occasionally? _____

Applicant may be asked the following questions:

How did you find out about the tutoring program?
What do you think is the cause of reading difficulty?
Why do you want to improve your reading?

Interviewers should advise applicants of the following:

After applications have been carefully considered, applicants will be assigned to
a volunteer tutor.
Applicants will be advised by mail of specific recommendations or
arrangements for participating in the tutoring program.

FORM D

Assignment Sheet

NAME OF STUDENT _____ AGE _____ DATE _____

ADDRESS OF STUDENT _____

READING LEVEL (Oral or silent reading tests; standardized or informal)

    Name of Test _____

    Score _____

Chief areas of difficulty:

If this student has special needs to be considered in scheduling, please be sure to summarize below (transportation, time, etc.):

Additional comments if necessary:

                                                                     _____
                                                                     Interviewer

Assigned to _____ Days _____ Time _____

Name _____ Place _____

Address _____

_____

Telephone No. _____

Lesson Plan

Tutor _____

Student _____

Date _____

Review

Readiness

Specific Purpose

General Purpose

Materials

Reading Selection: Title _____

Author _____

Source _____

Procedures

Evaluation

Contact Sheet

Date _____

Tutor _____

Student _____

Purpose

Materials used (including title and source of selection)

Procedures

Comments and/or reactions (tutor and student)

An Example of a Volunteer Program

The following description concerns general aspects of Literacy Volunteers of Long Island, Inc. This successful program is too comprehensive to discuss within the space limitations of this chapter; however, additional information can be obtained by writing to Ann DuPrey, Executive Director, 115 Nichols Court, Hempstead, Long Island, New York 11550.

The Need

About 28 percent of the adult population in Nassau County lack a high school diploma. And 40,000 read below the fifth grade level and can be classified as functional illiterates. In addition, many foreign adults have become part of the Nassau County community.

These individuals cannot read or write well enough to function effectively in our complex society, nor can they cope with everyday requirements for living—reading newspapers, signs, grocery labels, instructions, or obtaining a driver's license.

Thirteen years ago, a small but dedicated group of people recognized this need, sought to take action, and formed the nucleus of today's Literacy Volunteers of Long Island, Inc., an independent, not-for-profit affiliate of Literacy Volunteers of America, Inc. From the beginning, the organization has had one goal: To provide free reading instruction on a one-to-one basis to adults in need.

The Service: One-to-One Tutoring

One-to-one tutoring is an integral part of the LVLI program. It offers an alternative to traditional teaching methods and delivery systems, which, for many basic reading students, have become a treadmill of failure. And 50 percent of the English-as-a-Second Language students are illiterate in their native language. But a trained LVLI tutor is able to create the environment for success through positive reinforcement and application of tutoring methods proven to be effective. Tutors and students meet privately, for 2 sessions each week, at locations of their choice such as schools, homes, churches, or libraries. Trained tutors tailor basic reading and ESL lessons to the individual needs of their students. They help students to meet their goals and objectives.

In this one-to-one program of instruction, LVLI has helped over 2,700 adults in need, who have been referred from a variety of local health, religious, educational, and social service agencies.

The Training: Tutor Workshops

The essential element of the one-to-one tutoring service is the *volunteer* tutor. The strength of the tutor's approach is knowing how to use a variety of teaching techniques and how to personalize them to meet each student's needs and abilities.

Volunteer tutors learn this flexibility as part of the required Basic Reading Tutor Training Workshop or English-as-a-Second Language Tutor Training Workshop.

This course material is prepared by university reading specialists, working with the staff at the national Literacy Volunteers of

America, Inc. headquarters in Syracuse. These streamlined workshops utilize lectures, demonstrations, filmstrips and small group practice sessions. Experienced tutors act as leaders and course aids, training an average of 20 tutors at each workshop.

The workshops begin with an orientation session, followed by six classes of three hours each, scheduled over a three-week period in various Nassau County locations.

The Basic Reading and ESL Training and Standards Committees plan and offer ongoing advanced training courses for experienced tutors. Each tutor is required to attend at least one inservice training session per year. In addition to this formalized, structured program, specialists in various areas are readily available for consultation on an informal or as-needed basis.

The Behind the Scenes Structure

In 1968, a nucleus of volunteers began providing service as LVLI. Due to increased demands and because of its renowned reputation, LVLI became incorporated in 1978.

Since 1977 the Hempstead Public Library has been providing office space; the Nassau Library System provides services such as telephones, printing of flyers, books for tutors, and a small operating grant. LVLI depends on funding from a variety of governmental, corporate, and private agencies and individuals in addition to its funding from the New York State Education Department.

The complex needs of the organization could not be met, however, without those tutors whose work does not stop when the twice weekly lessons are completed. They chair or are members of committees which carry responsibility for workshop and inservice training, publicity, funding, instructional materials, LVLI library resources, and a newsletter.

As an affiliate of both the New York State and the national Literacy Volunteers organizations, LVLI is part of a nationwide movement to reduce illiteracy. It is currently one of the largest affiliates in New York State, providing guidance to the newer affiliates. On Long Island, the organization seeks to achieve the maximum results through increased support from residents, agencies, and businesses in the community.

Several suggestions for organizing and staffing the volunteer tutor program are described in the literature about adult literacy projects (*1, 2, 3*). A bibliography of materials suitable for use in adult literacy programs is particularly comprehensive (*4*). Another resource manual provides information about reading programs and systems expressly for adult basic education (*5*). Helpful guidance for leaders of a volunteer group, or program organizers, is available in a handbook (*6*). A service of Instructional Concept Guides and context units for supportive use by tutors can be adapted to any type of adult literacy program (*7*).

Evaluation of reading methods used to combat adult illiteracy suggests: a) The greater the use of varied materials the greater the flexibility for experimentation toward meaningful change (*8*). b) Both general reading and discreet reading subskills can be measured effectively through the use of several standardized reading tests (*9*). The language experience approach used with ESL adults provided opportunity for using students' literacy and survival level skills of their native language in learning to read and write in English (*10*).

The effectiveness of volunteer tutors in reading instruction has been described in reports of programs in Massachusetts (*11*), Ohio (*12*), Maryland (*13*), Nebraska (*14*), Georgia (*14*), Texas (*16*), and Oregon (*17*).

Practical help for the nonprofessional volunteer tutor during the past decade has been prepared in manual or booklet form as an available resource. Most of the publications were written to fill real needs which emerged with the development of the programs themselves (*18, 19, 20, 21, 22*). Direct guidance for teachers who train tutors emphasizes the tutor's role in the classroom as well as skills training (*23, 24*).

An overview of the reports of volunteer tutor programs reveals five points of emphasis:

1. *Age* of the client to be tutored
2. *Environment* or *setting* of instruction
3. *Material* of instruction and/or *approach* to teaching
4. *Sponsorship* of the program
5. *Purpose* of the program

A unique and successful approach in utilizing volunteers in a correctional institution was centered on a Learning Laboratory

Concept. Volunteers and interns were trained in prescriptive teaching of 8-14 year old boys (25).

In contrast to the confined setting, an educational television literacy effort in Britain included the volunteer sector as tutors (26).

Tutorial programs in a school setting have differed:

- A skills mastery plan, grades 1-3, as part of spp (Student Progress Plan) provided for improved promotion (27).
- A one-to-one relationship between tutor and 40 seventh graders resulted in a favorable impact on student self-concept (28).
- The effective use of tutors as mentors in a program for gifted readers has been documented (29).
- Parents as trained volunteer teacher aides were vital participants in a school reading program (30).
- Volunteer tutors have provided a better teacher-student ratio (31).
- Teen tutoring resulted in intrasubject and intersubject improvement for fourth and fifth graders (32).

With a single prevailing concept—the volunteer effort to improve literacy on a one-to-one relationship—numerous types of organizations have been developed. The reader is encouraged to adapt the suggestions offered in this chapter to meet individual or community needs. Additional references are included to provide a resource of information about the organization of volunteer tutor programs.

References
1. Smith, Carl B., & Leo C. Fay. *Getting People to Read: Volunteer Programs that Work*. New York: National Book Committee, 1973.
2. Eberwein, Lowell et al. "An Annotated Bibliography on Volunteer Tutoring Programs." Paper presented at the annual meeting of the Southeast Regional Reading Conference of the International Reading Association, 1976.
3. *Establishing Right-to-Read Programs in Community Based Adult Learning Centers*. Austin: Bureau of Industrial and Business Training, University of Texas at Austin.
4. Korkmas, Ann. *Adult Literacy: A Bibliography of Materials Suitable for Public Library Collections*. Dallas: Dallas Public Library, 1976.
5. *A Reading Program Resource Manual for Adult Basic Education*. Washington, D.C.: Clearinghouse for Offender Literacy Programs, American Bar Association, 1974.
6. Colvin, Ruth J.*LEADER: Literacy Education Assistance for the Development of Educational Resources. A Handbook for Organizers of Basic Reading Programs for Adults and Teenagers*. Syracuse, New York: Literacy Volunteers, 1972.
7. Palmatier, Robert A. et al. *Process and Product: A Guide for Assessment of Community Tutoring Programs,* Instructional Concept Guide No. 5. Athens, Georgia: Regional Adult Literacy Service Unit, University of Georgia, 1976.
8. *Teaching Adults to Read: Research and Demonstration in a Program of Volunteer Community Action*. Boston: Massachusetts Council for Public Schools, 1969.

9. Gold, Patricia Cohen, & Pamela L. Horn. "Achievement in Reading, Verbal Language, Listening Comprehension, and Locus of Control of Adult Illiterates in a Volunteer Tutorial Project," *Perceptual and Motor Skills, 54* (June 1982), 1243-1250.

10. Cohen, Judy et al. *A Reading and Writing Program Using Language Experience Methodology among Adult ESL Students in a Basic Education Program.* Washington, D.C.: Office of Vocational and Adult Education, 1981.

11. *Bourne Coordinated Total Reading Program.* Massachusetts: Bourne Union 10 School District, 1973.

12. *Early Reading Assistance: A Reading Tutorial Program.* Cleveland, Ohio: Program for Action by Citizens in Education, 1968.

13. *Evaluation of Project Upswing, Interim Report.* Silver Spring, Maryland: Operations Research, 1972.

14. *Multiple Activities Program ESEA Title I, September 1966 to September 1967: An Evaluation.* Lincoln, Nebraska: Nebraska State Department of Education, 1967.

15. *Urban Laboratory in Education: An Educational Improvement Project, Atlanta, Georgia, Annual Report, 1970-1971.* Atlanta, Georgia: Urban Lab in Education, 1971.

16. *The Fort Worth Plan: A Systems Approach for Continuous Progress in Reading for All Elementary Children.* Fort Worth, Texas: Fort Worth Public Schools, 1974.

17. Gaulke, Mary F. *Laubach Trained Volunteer Tutor Pilot Project 1971.* Medford, Oregon: Medford School District, 1972.

18. Tutors' Resource Handbook: Assessment Items and Sample Lessons. Washington, D.C.: Office of Education (DHEW), 1974.

19. Keene, Teresa. *Tips for Tutors: A Manual for Reading Improvement with 1973 Bibliographic Supplement.* Chicago: Chicago Public Library, 1973.

20. MacFarlane, Tom, & Donald Moyle (Eds.). *A Booklet for Volunteer Tutors.* Ormskirk, England: Edge Hill College of Education, 1974.

21. Sawyer, Diane J. "Preparing Volunteer Tutors," *Clearing House, 51* (December 1977), 152-156.

22. Laffey, James, & Phyllis Perkins. *Teacher Orientation Handbook.* Washington, D.C.: National Reading Center Foundation.

23. *Tutoring Resource Handbook for Teachers: A Guide for Teachers Who Are Working with Volunteer Reading Tutors.* Washington, D.C.: Office of Education (DHEW), 1974.

24. *Tutor-Trainers' Resource Handbook: Part A - Reading Directors' Organizational Guidelines; Part B - Tutor-Trainers' Guidelines; and Part C - Teacher-Orientation Guidelines.* Washington, D.C.: Office of Education (DHEW), 1974.

25. Mercantino, Anthony L. "A Volunteer Tutoring Program in Correctional Education: A Unique and Successful Approach in Utilizing Volunteers in a Learning Laboratory Program," *Journal of Correctional Education, 31* (September 1980), 19-20.

26. Richards, Maggie. "Britain Tackles Illiteracy," *Change, 10* (September 1978), 16-19.

27. *The Student Progress Plan (SPP) Implementation: Grades One-Three. Final Evaluation Report (School Year 1980-1981).* Washington, D.C.: District of Columbia Schools, 1981.

28. Banta, Trudy W., & Sandra S. Lawson. *Evaluation of the Lenoir City, Tennessee, School Power in Education Project, 1979-1980.* Knoxville: Bureau of Educational Research and Service, University of Tennessee, 1980.

29. Sanacore, Joseph. "Gifted and Talented Readers: The Hauppauge Plan," invited presentation at the Nassau Reading Council annual spring conference, Hofstra University, 1980.

30. Heimberger, Mary J. "Continued Focus on Families for Cultural Appreciation, Curriculum Planning, and Tutoring in Reading," paper presented at the Seventh IRA World Congress on Reading, Hamburg, West Germany, 1978.

31. Arundel, Anne. "PRIDE in Social Studies: Report of a Program Funded through ESAA, the Emergency Secondary Aid Act," paper presented at the Southeast Regional Meeting of the National Council for the Social Studies, New Orleans, Louisiana, 1976.

32. Klann, Harriet et al. *The Effects of Utilizing Teen Tutors in a Fourth and Fifth Grade Individualized Reading Program,* Research Report No. 143. Journal Announcement: RIEJUL 75.

Chapter 9
HELPFUL MATERIALS
FOR THE VOLUNTEER TUTOR*

Dolores Weissberg
Coney Island Hospital
Brooklyn, New York

This chapter focuses on materials for the volunteer tutor. The first two parts of the chapter consist of a column listing materials, a column indicating the general reading level of the materials, and a column suggesting the following age levels of students for whom the materials may be interesting:

C	child, ages 6-11
ET	early teens, ages 12-15
YA	young adult
A	adult
All	all ages

Materials Which Emphasize Readiness Skills, Word Analysis Skills, Vocabulary Development, and Spelling

	Reading Grade	Interest Level
The American Heritage School Dictionary. Houghton Mifflin	6 -9	All
Arco High School Equivalency Book. Arco Publishing Company	9+	YA,A
A Beginning Dictionary. Houghton/Mifflin	3 -6	C
Conquests in Reading. W. Kottmeyer & K. Ware. Webster Division, McGraw Hill	4 -8	C,ET,YA

*Based on a chapter from Guidelines to Teaching Remedial Reading by Lillie Pope (copyright 1975). Reprinted with permission of the publisher, Book-Lab. This section may not be reproduced without permission from the publisher.

	Reading Grade	Interest Level
Dr. Spello, W. Kottmeyer & K. Ware. Webster Division, McGraw Hill	4 -5	C,ET,YA
A First Course in Phonic Reading, L. Helson. Educators Publishing Service	Beg.	All
First Phonics, M. Burnett. Educators Publishing Service: Consonants, short vowels, supplemented by drill cards	Beg.	C,ET
Focus on Phonics, G. Rice. New Readers Press: Sequential development of phonic word attack skills	Beg. -5	ET,YA,A
Getting Ready to Read. W. Durr & R. Hillerich. Houghton Mifflin	Beg.	C
Glass-Analysis for Decoding Only, G. Glass. Walker Educational Book Corporation: Cluster packs plus follow through practice books	Beg. -6	All
Gould-Stern Early Reading Activities, T. Gould & M. Stern. Walker Educational Book Corporation: Kit A—Sound/symbol activities, Kit B—Decoding activities	Beg. -3	C
Hip Reader Books, C. Pollack & P. Lane. Book-Lab	Beg.	ET,YA,A
Intersensory Reading Program, C. Pollack. Book-Lab	Beg.	C,ET,YA
Laubach Way to Reading. New Readers Press: Sequential decoding skills and correlated readers	Beg. -5	YA,A
Learning Ways to Read Words, S. Feldman & K. Merrill. Teachers College Press	3 -6	All
Let's Read, A Linguistic Approach, C. Barnhart & L. Bloomfield. Wayne State University Press	1 -3	C,ET,YA
Lippincott Basic Reading. Harper & Row: A phonic linguistic approach	1 -6	C
McGraw-Hill Vocabulary, G. Stanford. Books 1-6, Webster Division, McGraw Hill	7+	ET,YA,A
Merrill Linguistic Reading Program. Charles E. Merrill Publishing: Books: A-K	Beg. -8	C,ET,YA
More Primary Phonics, B. Maker. Educators Publishing Service: Softcover storybooks and workbooks to supplement *Primary Phonics*	Beg.	C
My First Dictionary. Houghton Mifflin	Beg. -3	C
A New Time for Phonics, L. Scott. Webster Division, McGraw-Hill: Books A-F, sequential phonic skills	1 -3	C,ET
Open Court Correlated Language Arts Program. Open Court Publishing Company: Basic readers, workbooks, and supplementary storybooks stressing phonics approach	Beg. -6	C,ET
The Palo Alto Reading Program. Harcourt Brace Jovanovich: Sequential skills in reading	Beg. -3	C

Weissberg

	Reading Grade	Interest Level
Phonic Word Builder, Hy Ruchlis. Book-Lab	3 -8	All
Phonic Workbooks. Modern Curriculum Press: Sequential skills	1 -6	C,ET
Primary Phonics, B. Maker. Educators Publishing Service: Softcover storybooks and workbooks using short and long vowels	Beg.	C
Primary Readers Library. Modern Curriculum Press: Short vowels, long vowels, blends, and digraphs	1 -3	C
Programmed Phonics, L. Carroll. Educator's Publishing Service: Assumes some knowledge of initial and final consonant sounds	Beg.	All
Programmed Reading, Sullivan & Buchanan. Webster Division, McGraw Hill: Sequential decoding skills	Beg. -3	C
Programmed Reading for Adults. Webster Division, McGraw Hill	1 -6	ET,YA,A
Recipe for Reading Program, N. Traub. Walker Educational Book Corporation: Phonetic decoding storybooks	Beg. -6	C
Scholastic Practical English Program. Scholastic Book Services: Four volumes—1) grammar, 2) spelling and punctuation, 3) usage, 4) composition	9 -12	YA,A
Scott, Foresman Advanced Dictionary. Revised Edition of the Thorndike-Barnhart Advanced Dictionary. Doubleday & Company	9+	ET,YA,A
Sound Foundations Program. Developmental Learning Materials: Practice cards, presupposes a knowledge of consonants and consonant blends, starts with all five short vowels at once	Beg.	All
Sounds and Signals. Harper & Row: Five phonics workbooks, A-E	1 -3	C
Special Needs: Special Answers, L. Pope, D. Edel, & A. Haklay. Book-Lab	Beg. -6	C,ET
Spector Phonics. Leona Spector. Spector Associates	1 -4	All
SRA *Reading Program.* Science Research Associates	Beg. -6	C
Starting Off with Phonics. Modern Curriculum Press: Sequential skills	Beg. -3	C
Stories from Sounds. E. Hewetson, V. Shima. Educator's Publishing Service: Softcover storybooks using short vowels	Beg.	C
Teacher's Sampler. L. Pope, E. Edel, & A. Haklay. Book-Lab	Beg. -3	C
Thirty Days to a More Powerful Vocabulary, W. Funk & N. Lewis. Pocket Books	9+	YA,A
Thorndike Barnhart Handy Dictionary. Bantam	9+	YA,A

	Reading Grade	Interest Level
Vocabulary for the College Bound Student, H. Levin. AMSCO	9+	YA,A
Vowels and Stories, M. Weinstein. Book-Lab: Assumes a familiarity with consonants and consonant digraphs and a first grade vocabulary	2 -6	C,ET
Word Attack Series, S. Feldman. Teachers College Press	2 -4	All
Word Power Made Easy, N. Lewis. Pocket Books	9+	YA,A
Word Wealth, W. Miller. Holt, Rinehart & Winston	9+	YA,A
Wordly Wise, K. Hodkinson. Educators Publishing Service: Workbooks A,B,C and books 1-9	7+	ET,YA,A
World of Vocabulary, S.J. Rauch, Z. Clements, & A. Weinstein. Globe Book Company	2 -7	ET,YA

Materials to Develop Comprehension and Encourage Interest and Pleasure in Reading

	Reading Grade	Interest Level
Adult Learner Series, J. Green. Jamestown Publishers	2	YA,A
All in a Day's Work. Globe Book Company: 31 short nonfiction selections about different jobs	3	ET,YA
American Destiny Series. Book-Lab: Titles include history and biography—*Black Americans, Puerto Ricans, Jewish Americans*, and *Italian Americans*	3 -5	All
Americans. Garrard Publishing Company: Twenty-seven biographies (subjects include Pinkerton, W.C. Handy, etc.)	3 -6	All
Application Forms, B. Piltch. Frank E. Richards Publishing Company	3+	ET,YA,A
As a Child Grows, R. Keller. New Readers Press: Discipline and needs of young children	2+	YA,A
Banking, Budgeting, and Employment, A. Lennox. Frank E. Richards Publishing Company	3+	ET,YA,A
The Bank Street Readers. Macmillan	Beg. -3	C
Basic Skills in Reading Series, J. Sanacore. Cebco Standard Publishing: Six books emphasizing basic competency skills	4 -7	YA,A
Becoming a Driver, R. Grebel & P. Pogrund. Janus Book Publishers	2+	YA,A
Breakthrough Series, W.D. Sheldon et al. Allyn & Bacon	1 -6	ET,YA,A
Caring for a Child, M. Snowman. New Readers Press: Handbook on caring for preschool children	4+	YA,A

	Reading Grade	Interest Level
The Checkered Flag Series. Addison-Wesley	2+ -4+	C,ET,YA
Cloze Stories for Reading Success, H. Shangold. Walker Educational Book Corporation	1 -3	All
Cowboy Sam Series, Dan Frontier, and Sailor Jack. Benefic Press	Beg. -3	C
Critical Reading. Ann Arbor Publishers	4 -6	All
The Deep Sea Adventure Series. Addison-Wesley	1 -5	C,ET,YA
Discovery Books. Garrard Publishing Company: Biographies of famous people—Clara Barton, Mary McLeod Bethuen, Helen Keller	3	C
English 2200/English 2600/English 3200. Harcourt Brace Jovanovich: Short programed lessons in grammar and usage	7 -12	ET,YA,A
Every Reader Series, Classic Stories: Ben Hur, Call of the Wild. McGraw-Hill	1 -4	ET,YA
Famous Animal Stories. Garrard: Titles include *Balto, Sled Dog of Alaska; Captain, Canada's Flying Pony*	3	C
Finding a Good Used Car, W. Fletcher & P. Kelley. Janus Book Publishers	2+	YA,A
First Fact Books, Science Series. Lerner Publications	2	C
Follett Adult Basic Reading Comprehension Program. Cambridge Book Company	1 -3	YA,A
Garrard Sports Series. Garrard: Biographies of sports figures and sports histories	4	C,ET
Gates-Peardon-Laclair Reading Exercises. Teachers College Press: Books A-C	1 -7	C, ET
Getting Around Cities and Towns, W. Roderman. Janus Book Publishers	2+	ET,YA,A
Globe Adopted Classics. Globe Book Company: Includes titles such as *Tom Sawyer, Moby Dick, War of the Worlds*	3 -8	ET,YA
Globe Biography Collections. Globe Book Company: *Journeys to Fame, Turning Point, Profiles, Short World Biographies, Modern Short Biographies*	5 -6	All
Having a Baby, K. Koschnick. New Readers Press: Guide for parent-to-be	5+	YA,A
I Want a Job, M. Hudson & Ann A. Wearer. Frank E. Richards Publishing Company	3+	ET,YA
Jamestown Classics. Jamestown Publishers: Authors include: Edgar Allan Poe, O. Henry, Jack London, Bret Harte, Arthur Conan Doyle, and R.L. Stevenson	5	ET,YA,A
Janus Career Education Series. Janus Book Publishers: *Job Planner, My Job Application File,*		

	Reading Grade	Interest Level
Job Interview Guide, Time Cards and Paychecks, Get Hired, Don't Get Fired, Job Interview Kit	2+	ET,YA,A
Janus Money Matter Guides. Janus Book Publishers:*Master Your Money, Pay by Check, More for Your Money, Be Ad-Wise*	2+	ET,YA,A
Janus Survival Vocabulary Series. Janus Book Publishers: *Clothing Language, Drugstore Language, Job Application Language, Supermarket Language, Drivers License Language, Medical Language, Restaurant Language, Entertainment Language, Credit Language, Banking Language*	2	ET,YA,A
The Jim Forest Readers. Addison-Wesley	2 -7	C
Jobs from *A* to *Z*, Y. Dogin, Frank E. Richards Publishing Company	3+	ET,YA,A
Junior Science Books. Garrard Publishing Company: *Pond Life, Electricity, Icebergs and Glaciers, Light, Magnets, Bacteria, Rain, Hail, Sleet, and Snow, Stars, Water Experiences*	3	C
Landmark Books. Random House: Books of history and biography	4 -8	All
Laurel-Leaf Books. Dell Publishing: Paperback books, fiction and nonfiction for junior/senior high school	4 -7	ET,YA
Lerner Science Fiction Library. Lerner Publications	3 -4	C,ET,YA
The Look Book Series, E. Taylor. Educators Publishing Service: Nature readers on animals	3 -6	C
The Martin Mooney Mysteries, R. Monson & E. Johnston. Educator's Publishing Service	3 -4	C,ET,YA
McCall-Crabbs Standard Test Lessons in Reading. Teacher's College Press	2 -12	All
The Morgan Bay Mysteries. Addison-Wesley	2 -4	C,ET
Mystery Adventure Series. Benefic Press	2 -6	C,ET,YA
A Need to Read Series, S. Rauch & P. Trocki. Globe Book Company: Levels A, B, C, *Finding the Main Idea, Building Vocabulary, Identifying Details and Sequence, Drawing Conclusions, Critical Reading*	3 -6	ET,YA
New Practice Readers. Webster Division, McGraw-Hill, Books A-G	2 -6+	All
Occupations. New Readers Press: General job descriptions of 53 occupations	6+	YA,A
On Your Own. Janus Book Publishers: *Caring for Your Car, Need a Doctor? Getting Help, Sharing An Apartment*	2+	YA,A
Open Ended Plays, M. Velder et al. Globe Book Company	3 -4	ET,YA

	Reading Grade	Interest Level
Open Ended Stories, M. Velder & E. Cohen. Globe Book Company	4 -5	ET,YA
Out of Work, S. Ludwig. New Readers Press: Coping with unemployment, organizations, and programs supporting the unemployed	6+	YA,A
Pacemaker True Adventure Set. Fearon-Pitman	2	ET,YA
People Working Today Series. Janus Book Publishers: *Alex on the Grill, Bob the Super Clerk, Janet the Hospital Helper, Lester the Bellhop, Johnny at the Circuits, Julie at the Pumps, Kerry Drives a Van, Larry the Logger, Laura Cares for Pets, Tony the Night Custodian*	2+	YA,A
Pathways to the World of English, J. Abramowitz et al. Globe Book Company	5 -6	ET,YA
Personal Close-Ups, Biographies. Children's Press	3 -7	All
Preparing for a Job Interview, J. Wool. Frank E. Richards Publishing Company	3+	ET,YA,A
Racing Wheels Series. Benefic Press	2 -4	C,YA,ET
Reader Development Bibliography. New Readers Press: Philadelphia Free Library evaluation of books with readability levels for use with adults	2 -8	YA,A
Readers' Choice Catalogue. Scholastic Book Services: Inexpensive paperback books	2 -12	All
Reader's Digest Skill Builders, Reader's Digest Services	1 -8	All
Reader's Digest, Top Picks. Reader's Digest Services: Includes poems, plays, short stories, interviews; authors include O'Henry, Studs Terkel, Dore Schary	3-8	ET,YA,A
Reading about Science. Webster Division, McGraw-Hill: Books A-G.	2+ -6	All
Reading Development Kits. Addison-Wesley Publishing Company: Kit A, p-3; Kit B, 4-6; Kit C, 7-9	Beg. -9	YA,A
Reading Drills, E. Fry. Jamestown Publishers: Middle level, grades 4-6; advanced level, grades 7-10	4 -10	C,ET,YA
Reading for Concepts. Webster Division, McGraw-Hill: Books A-H	1+ -6+	All
Reading for Living. New Readers Press: Survival skills; signs, maps, writing letters, using telephones, using a dictionary	5 -7	ET,YA,A
Real Stories. Coronet	4 -5	All
Real Stories Series. Globe Book Company: Books A,B, 1,2	3 -6	ET,YA,A
Reluctant Reader Libraries. Scholastic Book Services	2 -8	ET,YA,A

	Reading Grade	Interest Level
Service Occupations, S. Throop & K. Hunter. Frank E. Richards Publishing	3+	ET,YA,A
Signal Books. Doubleday	4 -5	ET, YA
Sign Language: A Survival Vocabulary. Janus Book Publishers	2	ET,YA,A
Skill-by-Skill Workbooks. Modern Curriculum Press: *Getting the Main Idea, Following Directions, Increasing Comprehension, Organizing Information, Building Word Power, Working with Facts and Details, Using References*	2 -6	C,ET
Skimming and Scanning, E. Fry. Jamestown Publishers: Middle Level, grades 4-6; Advanced Level, grades 7-10	4 -10	C,ET,YA
Specific Skill Series. Barnell Loft, Ltd.: Books A-F are at grade levels one through six; after the first level, the books may be used by students of any age as remedial workbooks for improving comprehension skills	1 -6	All
Spectrum of Skills. Macmillan: Word analysis, vocabulary development, and reading comprehension	5+	ET,YA
Sports Mystery Series. Benefic Press	2 -4	C,ET,YA
Stranger than Fiction. Globe Book Company: Adapted news and magazine stories	3	ET,YA,A
Sundown Series, Leisure Reading Series. New Readers Press: Easy fiction for adults	2 -3	YA,A
Target Books. Garrard Publishing Company	3 -4	ET,YA
Teenage Tales. D.C. Heath & Company	3 -6	ET,YA
Using the Want Ads, W. Jew & C. Tandy. Janus Book Publishers	2+	YA,A
Walker Plays for Oral Reading, H. Gilford, Walker Educational Book Corporation	3 -4+	ET,YA,A
Weekly Reader. Weekly Reader Periodicals: Seven editions of curriculum based material—reading skills, current events, science and health, map skills, etc.	Beg. -6	C
The Wheels Series. New Readers Press: Titles include *Studying for a Drivers License* and *Becoming a Car Owner*	4+ -6	YA,A
World of Adventure Series, H. Bamman & R. Whitehead. Benefic Press	2 -6	ET,YA
Yearling Books. Dell Publishing Company: Paperback books of popular children's books by authors such as Judy Blume and Beverly Cleary, and the Yearling Biography Series which includes Abraham Lincoln, Louis Armstrong, & Buffalo Bill	2 -6	C,ET

Publishers and Suppliers of Games

Beckley-Cardy, 49 Main Street, Succasunna, New Jersey 07876
Developmental Learning DLM, DLM Park, Allen, Texas 75002
Educators Publishing Service, 75 Moulton Street, Cambridge, Massachusetts 02138
Garrard Press, 1607 N. Market Street, Champaign, Illinois 61820
Ideal School Supply Company, 11000 South Lavergne Avenue, Oaklawn, Illinois 60453
Instructo/McGraw-Hill, 18 Great Valley Parkway, Great Valley Corporate Center, Malvern, Pennsylvania 19355
Judy Company, 4325 Hiawatha Avenue, Minneapolis, Minnesota
Kenworthy Education Service, 138 Allen Street, Box 60, Buffalo, New York 14205
Lakeshore Curriculum Materials Company, Box 6261, Carson, California 90749
Lyons and Carnahan/Rand McNally, 23 East Madison, Chicago, Illinois
Milton Bradley Company, Springfield, Massachusetts 01101
New England School Supply, Box 1581, Springfield, Massachusetts 01101
Parker Brothers, Salem, Massachusetts 01102
Selchow and Righter Company, 200 Fifth Avenue, New York, New York 10010

Teaching Aids

Basic Sight Vocabulary Cards, E. Dolch, Garrard Publishing Company
Compound Words, Kenworthy Educational Service, Inc.
Consonant Blend Matching Cards, Montessori Matters and E-Z Learning Material
Consonant Blends, Kenworthy Education Service, Inc.
Consonant Wheels, Milton Bradley
Initial Consonant Matching Cards, Montessori Matters and E-Z Learning Material
Instant Spelling Deck, A. Cox, Educators Publishing Service, Inc.
Groovy Letters and Numbers, Wipe-off cards, Ideal.
Flannelboard Letters, Constructive Playthings
Informal Evaluation of Oral Reading Grade Level, Deborah Edel, Book-Lab
Kinesthetic Cards, Instructo/McGraw-Hill, flocked letter card
Kinesthetic Letters, Beaded Letters, Constructive Playthings
Letter Tracing Stencils, Constructive Playthings
Listening Aids through the Grades, D. Russell & E. Russell, Teachers College Press
Missing Letter Deck, A. Cox, Educators Publishing Service, Inc., alphabet sequence
My Puzzle Book, E. Dolch, Garrard Publishing Company, four books utilizing the Dolch basic sight vocabulary
Opposite Concepts, Instructo/McGraw-Hill
Phonetic Word Drill Cards, Kenworthy Educational Service, Inc.
Phonics for the Flannelboard, Instructo/McGraw-Hill, initial consonant substitution, final consonant blends, long and short vowels
Picture Word Cards, E. Dolch, Garrard Publishing Company

Pope-DiNola Word Bank, New Directions Press
Pope Inventory of Basic Reading Skills, L. Pope, Book-Lab, diagnostic test evaluating word attack skills in sequence
Prefixes, Kenworthy Educational Services, Inc.
Puppets, Childcraft, animals and people
Reading Aids through the Grades, D. Russell & E. Karp, Teachers College Press
Reading Development Bibliography, New Readers Press, 1982, lists books for adult beginning readers
Sentence Builder, Words and Phrases, Kenworthy Educational Service, Inc.
Short Vowel Picture and Word Matching Cards, Montessori Matters and E-Z Learning Material
Sight Phrase Cards, E. Dolch, Garrard Publishing Company
Suffixes, Kenworthy Educational Service
Syllable Flip Cards, Kenworthy Educational Service, Inc.
Tactile Letter Blocks, (Capitals and lowercase), Childcraft
Vowel Wheels, Milton Bradley
Wooden Alphabet Letters, Constructive Playthings

Periodicals

Action, Scholastic Book Services. Biweekly, reading levels grade 2-2.9; suitable for grades 7-9
Cobblestone, Cobblestone Publishing, Inc., 28 Main Street, Peterborough, New Hampshire 03458. A history magazine for young people
Ebony, Ebony Magazine, 820 S. Michigan Avenue, Chicago, Illinois 60605
Life, 541 N. Fairbanks Court, Chicago, Illinois 60611
National Geographic Magazine, 17 and M Streets NW, Washington, D.C. 20036
Natural History, American Museum of Natural History, 79 Street and Central Park West, New York, New York 10024
News for You, New Readers Press, Box 131, Syracuse, New York 13210 Weekly newspaper in two levels of difficulty, grades 4-5 and 5-6, of special interest to the young adult and adult reader
Popular Mechanics, Box 0062, Des Moines, Iowa 50374
Popular Science, Box 2516, Boulder, Colorado 80321
Scope, Scholastic Book Services. Weekly, reading levels grades 4-6, suitable for grades 8-12
Search, Scholastic Book Services, American History magazine, biweekly, reading levels grades 4-6, suitable for grades 8-12
Sprint, Scholastic Book Services, biweekly, reading level grades 2.0-2.9, suitable for grades 4-6

Background Reading for the Tutor

Guidelines for Teaching Children with Learning Problems, Lillie Pope, Book-Lab, 1982
Guidelines to Teaching Remedial Reading, Lillie Pope, Book-Lab, 1975
Growing into Reading, Marion Monroe, Greenwood Press, 1951
Helping Your Teenage Student, M. Cohen, Signet Books, 1979
How Children Fail, John Holt, Dell Publishing Company, 1970
How Children Learn, John Holt, Dell Publishing Company, 1970
Intelligence and Experience, J.M. Hunt, John Wiley and Sons, 1961
Language and Learning Activities for the Disadvantaged Child, G. Bereiter & S. Engelmann, Antidefamation League of the B'nai B'rith
The Lives of Children, George Dennison, Random House, 1969
No Easy Answers: The Learning Disabled Child, S. Smith, Houghton Mifflin, 1979
Primer for Parents, Paul McKee, Houghton Mifflin
Teacher, S. Ashton-Warner, Bantam Books, 1963
Teaching Reading to Adults, Edwin Smith & Marie Smith, Monarch Press, 1975
Teaching Reading, Writing, and Study Strategies: The Content Areas, H.A. Robinson, Allyn and Bacon, 1983
Tutor: A Handbook for Tutorial Programs, Lillie Pope, Book-Lab, 1976
Using Language Experience with Adults, Kennedy & Roeder, New Readers Press, 1975
Using Readability, Laubach & Koschnick, New Readers Press, 1977, a guide for writing or evaluating materials for adults
What Every Parent Should Know about Learning Disabilities, Channing L. Bete Company
When You Teach English as a Second Language, Constance Jolly & Robert Jolly, Book-Lab, 1974

Directory of Publishers

Addison-Wesley Publishing Company, Sand Hill Road, Menlo Park, California 94025
Allyn and Bacon, Inc., Link Drive, Rockleigh, New Jersey 07647
American Book Company, 135 West 50 Street, New York, New York 10020
American Technical Publishers, Inc., 12235 S. Laramie Avenue, Alsip, Illinios 60658
AMSCO School, 315 Hudson Street, New York, New York 10013
Ann Arbor Publishers, Box 388, Worthington, Ohio 43085
Antidefamation League of B'nai B'rith, 823 United Nations Plaza, New York, New York 10017
Arco Publishing, Inc., 215 Park Avenue South, New York, New York 10003
Association for Library Service to Children, 50 E. Huron Street, Chicago, Illinois 60611
Bantam Books, Inc., 666 Fifth Avenue, New York, New York 10019

Barnell, Loft Ltd., 958 Church Street, Baldwin, New York 11510

Beckley-Cardy Company, 114 Gaither Drive, Mt. Laurel, New Jersey 08054

Bell and Howell Company, 801 Second Avenue, New York, New York 10003

Benefic Press, 1250 Sixth Avenue, San Diego, California 92101

Bobbs-Merrill Company, Box 7080, 3200 W. 62 Street, Indianapolis, Indiana 46206

Book-Lab, 500 74 Street, North Bergen, New Jersey 07047

Bowman-Noble Publishers, Inc., 4563 Colorado Boulevard, Los Angeles, California 90039

Brookes, Paul H. Publishing Company, Box 10624, Baltimore, Maryland 21204

Cambridge Book Company, 888 Seventh Avenue, New York, New York 10106

Chandler and Sharp Publishers, Inc., 11A Commercial Boulevard, Novato, California 94947

Channing L. Bete Company, Inc., South Deerfield, Maine 01373

Childcraft, 20 Kilmer Road, CN 066, Edison, New Jersey 08818

Children's Press, 1224 W. Van Buren Street, Chicago, Illinois 60607

Compton, F.E. and Company, 425 N. Michigan Avenue, Chicago, Illinois 60611

Constructive Playthings, 2008 West 103 Terrace, Leawood, Kansas 66206

Continental Press, Inc., 520 East Bainbridge Street, Elizabethtown, Pennsylvania 17022

Coronet, The Multimedia Company, 65 E. South Water Street, Chicago, Illinois 60601

Creative Editions, Box 22246, Sacramento, California 95822

Crowell, Thomas Y., Company, 10 East 53 Street, New York, New York 10022

Dell Publishing Company, 1 Dag Hammarskjold Plaza, New York, New York 10017

Denoyer-Geppert Company, 5235 N. Ravenswood Avenue, Chicago, Illinois 60640

Developmental Learning DLM, Inc., One DLM Park, Allen, Texas 75002

Dexter and Westbrook, Ltd., 958 Church Street, Baldwin, New York 11510

Doubleday and Company, 501 Franklin Avenue, Garden City, New York 11530

Dover Publications, Inc., 180 Varick Street, New York, New York 10014

Educational Activities, 1937 Grand Avenue, Baldwin, New York 11510

Educational Performance, 600 Broad Avenue, Ridgefield, New Jersey 07657

Educational Teaching Aids, 159 West Kinzie, Chicago, Illinois 60610

Educators Publishing Service, 75 Moulton Street, Cambridge, Massachusetts 02138

Encyclopedia Britannica Educational Corporation, 425 N. Michigan Avenue, Chicago, Illinois 60611

English Language Services, Inc., Division of Washington Educational Research Association, Buckingham Parkway, Culver City, California 90230

Fearon-Pitman Learning, Inc., Six Davis Drive, Belmont, California 94002

Ferguson, J.G., Publishing Company, 111 E. Wacker Drive, Chicago, Illinois 60601

Field Enterprises Educational Publications, Division of World Book, Inc., Merchandise Mart Plaza, Room 510, Chicago, Illinois 60654

Follett Publishing Company, 1010 West Washington Boulevard, Chicago, Illinois 60607

Garrard Publishing Company, 1607 N. Market Street, Chicago, Illinois 61820

Greenwood Press, 88 Post Road West, Box 5007, Westport, Connecticut 06881

Ginn and Company, 191 Spring Street, Lexington, Massachusetts 02173

Globe Book Company, 50 West 23 Street, New York, New York 10010

Hammond, Inc., 515 Valley Street, Maplewood, New Jersey 07040

Harcourt Brace Jovanovich, Inc., 757 Third Avenue, New York, New York 10017

Harper and Row Publishers, 10 East 53 Street, New York, New York 10022

Heath, D.C., and Company, 125 Spring Street, Lexington, Massachusetts 02173

Holt, Rinehart and Winston, 383 Madison Avenue, New York, New York 10017

Houghton Mifflin Company, One Beacon Street, Boston, Massachusetts 02108

Ideal School Supply Company, 11000 South Lavergne Avenue, Oak Lawn, Illinois 60453

Instructo, McGraw-Hill, 18 Great Valley Parkway, Great Valley Corporate Center, Malvern, Pennsylvania 19355

Irwin, Richard D., Inc., 1818 Ridge Road, Homewood, Illinois 60430

Jamestown Publishers, Box 6743, Providence, Rhode Island 02940

Janus Book Publishers, 2501 Industrial Parkway West, Hayward, California 94545

Judy Company, 4325 Hiawatha Avenue, Minneapolis, Minnesota 55406

Kenworthy Educational Service, Inc., Box 60, 138 Allen Street, Buffalo, New York 14205

Lakeshore Curriculum Materials Company, Box 6261, Carson, California 90749

Lerner Publications, Lerner Publishing Company, 241 First Avenue North, Minneapolis, Minnesota 55401

Lippincott, J.B., Company, East Washington Square, Philadelphia, Pennsylvania 19105

Love Publishing Company, 1777 South Bellaire Street, Denver, Colorado 80222

Loyola University Press, 3441 N. Ashland Avenue, Chicago, Illinois 60657

Lyons and Carnahan, Rand McNally, 23 East Madison, Chicago, Illinois

McCormick-Mathers Publishing Company, 135 West 50 Street, New York, New York 10019

McGraw-Hill, Inc., 1221 Avenue of the Americas, New York, New York 10020

McKay, David, Inc., Two Park Avenue, New York, New York 10016

Macmillan Company, 866 Third Avenue, New York 10022

Merrill, Charles E., Books, Inc., 1300 Alum Creek Drive, Columbus, Ohio 43216

Modern Curriculum Press, 13900 Prospect Road, Cleveland, Ohio 44136

Monarch Press, 1230 Avenue of the Americas, New York 10020

Montessori Matters and E-Z Learning Materials, 701 East Columbia Avenue, Cincinnati, Ohio 45215

National Association for Public Continuing and Adult Education, 1201 Sixteenth Street NW, Washington, D.C. 20036

National Textbook Corporation, 8259 Niles Center Road, Skokie, Illinois 60077
New Directions Press, R.D. 4, Newton, New Jersey 07826
New Readers Press, Box 131, Syracuse, New York 13210
New York University Press, Washington Square, New York, New York 10003
Open Court Publishing Company, 1058 Eighth Street, LaSalle, Illinois 61301
Orton Dyslexia Society, 8415 Bellona Lane, Towson, Maryland 21204
Parker Brothers, Inc., 200 Fifth Avenue, New York, New York 10003
Pendulum Press, Inc., Saw Mill Road, West Haven, Connecticut 06516
Pitman Learning, Inc., 6 Davis Drive, Belmont, California 94002
Pocket Books, Division of Simon and Schuster, 1230 Avenue of the Americas, New York, New York 10020
Prentice-Hall, Inc., Educational Book Division, Englewood Cliffs, New Jersey 07632
Putnam Publishing Group, 200 Madison Avenue, New York, New York 10016
Rand McNally and Company, 8255 Central Park Avenue, Skokie, Illinois 60076
Random House, 201 East 50 Street, New York 10022
Reader's Digest Services, Educational Division, Pleasantville, New York 10570
Richards, Frank E., Publishing Company, Box 66, Phoenix, New York 13135
S & S Arts and Crafts, Colchester, Connecticut 06415
Schaffer, Frank, Publications, 19771 Magellan Drive, Torrance, California 90202
Scholastic Book Services, 906 Sylvan Avenue, Englewood Cliffs, New Jersey 07632
Science Research Associates, Inc., 155 N. Wacker Drive, Chicago, Illinois 60606
Scott, Foresman and Company, 1900 E. Lake Avenue, Glenview, Illinois 60025
Scribner's, Charles, Sons, 597 Fifth Avenue, New York, New York 10017
Selchow and Righter Company, 200 Fifth Avenue, New York, New York 10010
Signet Books, The New American Library, 1633 Broadway, New York, New York 10019
Silver Burdett Company, 250 James Street, Morristown, New Jersey 07960
Simon and Schuster, 1230 Avenue of the Americas, New York, New York 10020
Society for Visual Education, Inc., 1345 Diversey Parkway, Chicago, Illinois 60614
South-Western Publishing Company, 5101 Madison Road, Cincinnati, Ohio 45227
Spector Associates, 445 E. 14 Street, New York, New York 10009
Steck-Vaughan Company, Box 2028, Austin, Texas 78768
Teachers College Press, Columbia University, Teachers College, 1234 Amsterdam Avenue, New York, New York 10027
Teaching Resources Corporation, 50 Pond Park Road, Hingham, Massachusetts 02043
United Educators, Inc., Tangley Oaks Educational Center, Lake Bluff, Illinois 60044
United States Government Printing Office, Washington, D.C. 20025
University of Chicago Press, 5801 Ellis Avenue, Chicago, Illinois 60637
Veritas Publications, Box 4418, Arlington, Virginia 22204

Viking Press, 40 West 23 Street, New York, New York 10010

Walker Educational Book Corporation, 720 Fifth Avenue, New York, New York 10019

Washington Square Press, Division of Simon and Schuster, 1230 Avenue of the Americas, New York, New York 10020

Wayne State University Press, 5959 Woodward Avenue, Detroit, Michigan 48202

Webster Division, McGraw-Hill Book Compnay, 1221 Avenue of the Americas, New York, New York 10020

Wiley, John, and Sons, 605 Third Avenue, New York, New York 10158

Weekly Reader Periodicals, 1250 Fairwood Avenue, Box 16626, Columbus, Ohio 43216

Xerox Education Publications, 1250 Fairwood Avenue, Columbus, Ohio 43216